THE FORTY SERVANTS
LITTLE BLACK BOOK.

ARTWORK AND TEXT BY
TOMMIE KELLY

Copyright © 2018 by Tommie Kelly
All rights reserved.

This book, including all text and artwork, or any portion thereof may not be reproduced or used in any manner whatsoever without the express written permission of the creator except for the use of brief quotations in a book review.

First Printing, 2018

www.AdventuresInWooWoo.com
www.TheFortyServants.com
www.TommieKelly.com

ISBN-13: 978-1722873769
ISBN-10: 1722873760

ACKNOWLEDGMENTS

A big thank you to all my test readers: Michael Metelits, Jerome Madulid, Vanessa Irena, Lua Valentia, Lea Akiona, Marcelo Bueno, and Siddhi Sahaja Arciniega.

A huge thank you to Robbie Laliberte and Michael Metelits for proofreading and editorial assistance.

A big thanks to Josh Horton for the Map Magick idea and to Michael Metelits for the Spirits of Place suggestion.

I would like to give a huge thanks to The Forty Servants Facebook groups for all their insights, feedback and generous sharing of their experiences with the Servants. I also want to thank everyone who has sent me a message or email telling me all about their experiences with the Servants. All of your insights helped me in writing this book.

I also want to thank my wife Venessa for continuing to put up with me.

For all details on how to purchase The Forty Servants Deck, Altar Cards and Images, or the Digital Deck and to get all the latest information please go to:

www.TheFortyServants.com

WHAT ARE THE FORTY SERVANTS?

Firstly, The Forty Servants are forty individual archetypes, ideas or representations of energies that can be used for divination purposes. For example, you can shuffle the deck, pick out cards, and then lay them out in a predetermined spread. By analysing a card's position in the spread and then looking up what that card represents you can gain some insight into the question asked.

Secondly, The Forty Servants can also be used in your day to day life to increase or decrease the amount of energy or influence that each Servant represents. This is known in some circles as magick, but it goes by many names.

You can use The Forty Servants exclusively for divination, or exclusively for magick, or you can use them for both, it's totally up to your own needs and preferences. If divination doesn't interest you then the magick side will still serve you just as well, and the opposite also holds true.

But the above descriptions are only of their uses and not of their nature. So, what exactly are The Forty Servants?

At the outset I had a very definite answer to what the exact nature of the Servants was: "The Forty Servants are servitors"; but these days I am not so sure. These days it's hard to pinpoint exactly what they are, and the more I try, the more I get the feeling that I am somehow missing the point, and in many ways I am only limiting them by trying.

But defining a servitor is as good a place as any to begin, so let's start there.

A servitor is commonly described as a thought-form. Personally though, I prefer to see a servitor as *an idea*. Servitors are created in order to fulfill a particular purpose or perform a certain function. So in our case, each of The Forty Servants has been given a particular role, or power, so that they can be used to aid or guide you. Some Servants represent protection, or increased good luck, while others impart wisdom and knowledge, some are for personal development and many other things.

But what does a servitor or thought-form look like in day to day life? Are servitors alive? Are they spirits? Do they have a mind and will of their own? Can you see them? Can other people see them? Well, sadly, there are no definitive answers to these questions. Everyone will have a different experience and view on servitors. I personally know people who have physically seen their own, or other people's, servitors, I know people who can sense a presence or even hear a voice. I also know people who have never seen, felt or heard their servitors but use them anyway as they seem to be quite effective. And others still, never seem to get servitors to work no matter what they try. I have yet to see any of The Forty Servants in the mundane world, though some people have told me that they have.

The Forty Servants were created by me during the period of late spring to autumn of 2016. I did all the artwork, wrote the original guidebook (poorly I will add), designed the box, formatted the art for the printers, made the websites and groups, and basically did all the things that a creator of a piece of art would do. I did all the mundane things but I also wanted them to be functional servitors that other people could use, and this required an extra step in the process of creation. This is where the woo woo comes in.

The Servants were finally complete and *birthed* on Halloween Night, 2016 in a special ceremony which involved, among other things, me blowing life into each of them, anointing them with ritual oil and giving them representations of each of the classical elements. It was at this point that they became more than just interesting lifeless pictures.

I then let them loose out into the world, thinking that maybe a handful of people would find them interesting or useful. After all, The Forty Servants were mainly created because *I* wanted to use and have them as part of my magick work. I really didn't expect many other people to care that much about them.

But then a curious thing happened- lots and lots of people became interested in them, and it quickly became obvious that The Forty Servants were on a journey of their own- a journey that I could never have imagined!

I am extremely proud of my work on the Servants; it flowed out of me almost as if I was just the channel rather than the creator – but don't get me wrong, I certainly wouldn't go so far as to say this is channeled work. However, at times, it really did feel like other hands were at work alongside me or that there was a bigger picture to the story that I wasn't fully privy to. It reminded me of when I was writing **THEM** and **THE HOLY NUMBERS** – there was a point where the characters took over and I became as much a witness to the story unfolding as the readers were. The difference is that the reader didn't have to get up every morning and actually do the writing and drawing, and I most certainly did.

When I was working on The Servants' images I felt somewhat like a sculptor who had to chip away at the stone until the statue revealed itself, rather than me forcing my own ideas on the stone.

From the start there was a feeling that The Servants had a life of their own, and they also seemed to have a purpose: one which is probably better known to them than me. I guess in hindsight it seems appropriate to say that The Servants found me, rather than I found them. If you are a creator of any kind then I am quite sure you understand exactly what I mean when I say this.

One of the main reasons I wanted to create the Servants was to give myself, and other like-minded people, simple and easy access to certain helpful archetypal models and energies. Therefore, the Servants can be viewed as representations of the original energies and ideas that have existed since time began. The word archetype comes from the Greek words *arkhe* meaning "original" or "first principle" and *typos* which means "model" or "copy". So, The Forty Servants represent these original ideas and therefore can throw some light on our questions or queries in a divination. However, they also have the added element of being available and useful in day to day life.

Some of the Servants have very obvious influences from known spirits: Ganesha in the Road Opener, Papa Legba in the Gate Keeper, or Saint Cyprian in The Saint; but they are not these actual spirits. They are similar in nature, and borrow energy and attributes from the spirits but they are not the *actual* spirit. Instead they are a way to easily and simply access the same power and energy that this spirit represents without the need to involve yourself in the system the spirit originates from.

Traditionally, servitors need to be "fed" to continue to exist. The Forty Servants were created to live and feed on attention and their use by people. The more attention they receive the more powerful they will become for everyone who uses them. However, it is important to note that what someone does with the Servants has no impact on anyone else, save for the fact that it adds to the overall power level of the Servants. Someone doing something "bad" or "good" with the Servants does not add to anyone else's karma or similar (that is, of course, if karma is even an idea you subscribe to). Being fed by attention means that The Forty Servants are totally reliant on humans to exist. If people stop using them or thinking about them they will cease to be.

An egregore is similar to a servitor but it has been created by a group of people, and over time it becomes an autonomous entity made up of, and influencing, the thoughts of the group. While creation by a group is the usual method, if enough people put energy or belief into someone else's servitor, it would likely become an egregore given enough time and group usage.

While The Forty Servants could be seen to fall under the category of egregores, I am hesitant to use the word or give them this label. The problem comes with the word "autonomous". The thought of the Servants running wild and free scares people and puts some off using the system altogether.

To this I say: first and foremost the Servants work for you. Their function is to serve you and help you get the things you want. The whole point of The Forty Servants was to give people easy, safe and direct access to the energy and power of these archetypes.

This is the whole beauty of the Servants. They are here to help and serve you. This is what they were created for. So, if you ever find that they appear to be running rampant and causing havoc it is because you have let them or want them to on some level. At some point *you* gave them license to run free.

While there are internet reports of servitors getting out of control, most of these reports that I have come across are from people whose lives already seem a bit out of control or where drama already seems to follow them around. I personally have never had a servitor get out of hand or anything even close to that.

The best way to think of the relationship is that you are the employer, and the Servants the employees. You are the boss and the Servants work for you. You can be a good and kind boss if you want, but you must be the boss. The Servants were created to serve, and they are very happy to do so. Aim to stay in control at all times and keep the proper balance of this relationship in place.

Now finally, there is also a case to be made that suggests that The Forty Servants are just ideas in the user's head and nothing more. It's not magick, it's not woo woo, it's all psychological. It's all just in our heads. But this doesn't mean that The Forty Servants are useless or have no power.

In this theory The Forty Servants allow people to tap into their own minds and allow them to feel what it would be like to be each of the archetypal energies. For instance, we can *invoke* The Father Servant and start to imagine what he must feel like, or be like. How does he think? What would his inner dialogue sound like? How would he approach a problem? We could then go out into the world from this unique perspective. The same goes for any of The Servants – for example The Healer has the ability to engage the placebo response. If we approach the world from a certain view point the world tends to mirror that back to us. From this physiological view point alone, using The Forty Servants can be extremely powerful and beneficial in many ways.

In the end, I think it is best to leave the answer of "What Exactly Are The Forty Servants?" to each user to decide for themselves. Are they spirits? Are they servitors? Are they egregores? Are they archetypes? Is it all just in our heads? Are they a mix of all of these things?

And perhaps it doesn't matter what they are, only that they work.

WHAT IS DIVINATION?

Divination is a process to find out something you don't know by way of a special ritual. For example, diviners read cards, throw dice, read tea leaves, notice signs, events, omens, or contact a supernatural agency such as the dead. But there are a host of other ways, systems and paths; loads of them and particular divination methods vary by culture and religion.

Divination is not quite fortune-telling though, as that's just concerned with predicting the future. Divination, however, can be used to gain insight into the past, present or future.

Does It Work?
Like all magick, divination seems to work ridiculously well sometimes and then not at all at other times. There doesn't seem to be any great explanation for why this is, but this is pretty much

the exact experience of any divinator I have spoken to.

Perhaps sometimes it's simply just the wrong time to do it. When you are stressed or anxious you probably won't see the answers as easily as when you are relaxed and calm. But, this is just one example - there are lots of factors, known and unknown, that are involved.

For me personally, I find divination works best when you are trying to work out your thoughts or feelings on present situations or to unravel events of the past. In my experience, and in that of other people I have talked to, divination is less reliable when predicting the future, although not totally useless.

That said, divination can be successful in gauging what the most likely outcome to your current situation is. Patterns can be recognised that point to the probability of certain future events occurring. However, the Catch-22 is that now that you have this information about the probable future outcome, you have already started to change it.

The traditional advice given is to aim to only perform divinations for the short-term future. The more you travel into the far future the less accurate the reading will be. But you should experiment for yourself and find out what works best for you and your abilities. You just might have the gift for perfect future prediction and who I am to keep you from that role.

Despite a long history of use, divination is now often dismissed by the scientific community and skeptics as being nothing more than superstitious nonsense. Most of the fortune-telling in the media, books, films and on TV is rubbish. There are also many frauds and charlatans out there who really are just in it to make money or get attention.

Not all, though, and we shouldn't rush to judgment on the system as a whole just because of some bad apples. I personally don't think divination should be dismissed. It really can be a brilliant tool if used wisely. I suggest you view divination as a helpful second opinion look at events in your life that can help to make sense of things going on around you. The cards may assist you to look at proceedings from a different angle or perspective. The cards could trigger something in your mind that may lead you to form different ideas, find solutions, or make you see things in a new light.

Doing a Reading

This is really down to personal taste and so I don't want to say that there is only one way to use the deck. The more you use the deck the more you will find out what works for you and what doesn't. The goal is to find the best system for you, so try a number of spreads and ideas and then settle on the ones that work and feel best for each different situation.

My own favorite and the spread I use almost exclusively is a three card reading. You simply ask the question, out loud or in your mind, shuffle the deck and then randomly pick out three cards – one for the Past, one for the Present, and the last one for the Future.

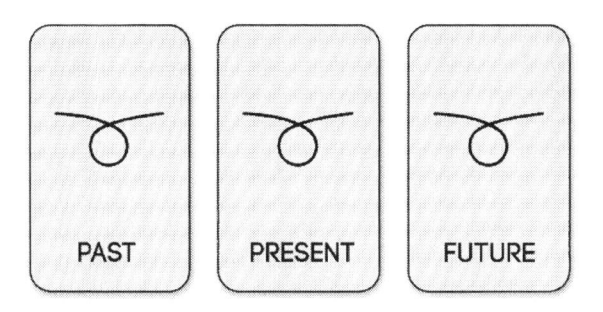

| PAST | PRESENT | FUTURE |

Another method is to ask "What do I need to know right now?" or "What is my best next move?" or something similar, and then pick out one card randomly from the deck. Although very simple, this is a surprisingly effective method. You can also employ a two card version with the first card is "DO THIS", and the second card is "DON'T DO THIS".

While The Forty Servants is not a Tarot deck, you can still utilize the well-known Tarot spreads in your readings. A quick Google search will find a host of Tarot spreads for you to try out.

A quick warning about reading for yourself - you can be too close to some situations to really get an objective view on it so you might be better served to have someone else do the reading for you. Always keep this in mind when doing personal readings.

And remember you are not limited to just doing readings for yourself. You can do great readings for other people with this deck.

All the methods and card layouts are the same, just get the other person to ask the questions, shuffle the deck and pick the cards.

Reversals

Reversals are when the card is turned over and the image lands upside down. In tarot, and some oracle decks, this is often seen a sign to read the card as the opposite of what it normal means. Personally I don't use reversals--that's just not how the Forty Servants system was designed to be used. Most cards have both good and bad aspects to them and a lot of the cards already have an opposite card (The Carnal and The Chaste, or The Seer and The Thinker) which makes reversal a bit redundant.

Some cards will lend themselves to being read as reversed but some won't. So maybe the best approach is to take it on a case by case basis.

Everyone has their own style and I wouldn't want to curb that by making some sort of NO REVERSALS rule. If you want to use them – use them, but I bet you find that it often just doesn't work.

WHAT IS MAGICK?

One of the first questions that people ask on occult forums and discussions boards is: "what exactly is magick?'" For the answer we can look to many sources who have tried to give a clear, precise and working definition of what it is.

Aleister Crowley defined magick as: "the

science and art of causing change to occur in conformity with will" and later added that "every intentional act is a magical act." **Donald Michael Kraig** changed this to: "magick is the science and art of causing change (in consciousness) to occur in conformity with will, using means not currently understood by traditional western science." **Gordon White** sees magick as "probability enhancement," and **Alan Chapman** believes "magick is the art of experiencing truth." but he also very correctly states that "there isn't a man, woman or child on this planet that does not know what magick is."

Someone, somewhere, and for the life of me I can't remember who, defined it as "**the art of getting lucky on purpose**." If you know who said this, please email me and let me know, as it is the definition I enjoy the most.

There is something very primal, ancient, and mysterious about magick. We recognise it immediately when we see it, or more likely when we *feel* it occurring around us or when we stumble into its aftermath. Just like walking into a room and knowing that the people have been arguing by the feel of the air, we can sense magick by the aura it leaves behind. But you have to be careful, it's all too easy to dismiss it.

Is Magick Real?

To me, this is somewhat the wrong question. The better question is: **is it useful**? Besides, what exactly is "real"? Statistically, it appears, or at least it is currently fashionable to suggest, we are more likely to be living in a computer simulation than in base or "true" reality. So our ideas of what we consider "real" may be quite foolish when looked at from a perspective higher than our own.

If you don't believe in it then there is nothing anyone can do or say that will change your mind. Therefore any argument I would make is pointless. So just close this book and we'll all happily go our own ways.

My assertion has always been: does following the techniques, practices, ideas, systems and rituals of magick lead me closer to health, happiness, satisfaction, prosperity, creativity, contentment and wisdom? If the answer is yes, then we should keep them. If the answer is no, then we should change the approach or just drop them altogether.

The occult and magickal practices and ideas that have worked best and most consistently for me are the ones that I have developed and shaped into The Forty Servants system.

Does Magick Work?

Just like divination, magick works **unbelievably** well at times and absolutely not at all at other times even with all factors being equal. However, there is an often touted "get out clause" that purports that magick **always** works - just not in the way you wanted or expected.

For instance, you do magick to win the lottery but you don't win it. If magick is just probability enhancement, then the magick worked perfectly - it's just that it lowered your odds from 50 million to 1, to 25 million to 1. A huge feat in itself, but ultimately of no help to you whatsoever.

While interesting, this "always works" theory is totally unfalsifiable and therefore, for me, it's a bit unhelpful. I prefer to just say it did or didn't work. Seems more direct and simple to me.

When it works, you'll know it has worked. **You feel it.** But be careful, very quickly afterwards, the world tries to normalise the event. The magick event seems to become less and less magick as time goes on or the more you think about it. Rational thought creeps in and convinces you of some mundane explanation. Eventually you doubt the whole experience and then reject the idea completely.

This is why it is very important to keep a magickal diary where you write down all the details of your successes and failures. Keep records of your readings, your rituals and describe your experiences. Take special note of the feeling when you know the magick has worked – don't let your rational mind try to convince you that anything other than magick was at play.

People often dismiss the whole phenomenon of thinking about someone and then they phone you, or you meet them, or something similar. Skeptics say that we think about people all the time and when nothing unusual happens and we just forget about it. We only remember the times when something weird occurs and then we convince ourselves that some sort of ESP has occurred.

There probably is a lot of truth in this, but I don't totally buy it. When these things happen **it**

feels radically different. I have often thought of people and not have them ring me afterwards, we all have, but when one of these special experiences happens the whole **feeling** is different. It's just not the same **at all** as casually thinking of someone. It's a very unique feeling - and to me this weird (or even wyrd) feeling is what magick feels like.

And when your magick doesn't work, you just try again - there really does seems to be a bit of a practice element to it. Skeptics sometimes will say that magick only works when you believe in it. But I think this is slightly the wrong way round. Magick only doesn't work when you don't believe in it. It's the active Non-belief that stops it working. Not caring, not knowing or being a total believer all seem to work just as well. Non-belief manages to severely limit it though.

As does worrying or fretting about whether it will work or not. Occultists often talk about removing "lust of result" but I don't totally gel with that expression as it implies you can't *want* something and then still get it. Or that it's the act of "wanting" itself which stops you from getting the thing you want. I don't believe that as I have gotten plenty of things I really wanted.

I feel the bigger factor in failure than the "lust of result" is the **worry** that you won't get what you want rather than the **wanting** itself. So, I say: want away! Just chill on worrying about it not happening as this has the potential to kill your magick. When you are convinced that something magickal will happen, it usually does.

As always though, your mileage may vary.

Sigils

Sigils are an inscribed or painted symbol considered to have magical power. Each Servant has a unique sigil that can be used to activate the corresponding energy or archetype in your ritual work. These symbols can be used at any time; you don't have to have the Servant images in front of you to avail yourself of their power and magick. You can draw the sigils in the air in front of you, on paper and carry them with you, or even draw them on to your body.

If you want to know more about Sigils in general then you can check out my blog where I have a detailed post about them:
http://bit.ly/woosigils

THE RITUALS

The First Step
Before you read anything about what the Servants represent, or what their powers are, spend some time looking at their images and see what insights come to you about them. Let your mind relax and try to release any preconceived notions you may have about the names, labels or archetypes the Servants represent. Just let them speak to you through their images and then write down any details about the Servants that come to mind.

Some people report getting special names for each Servant that are unique to them, while others find that they feel that they have known particular Servants for years already.

This is an important step and often leads to great insights and understanding. Of course, if nothing comes to mind that's perfectly fine too. Everyone's experience will be different.

The Box Burning
A trend appeared very soon after The Forty Servants entered the world: people felt compelled to burn the cardboard box in which the Servant cards arrived. The cards were then placed in their new home such as a wooden box, a cloth bag or similar.

This act has become so popular, that I felt I needed to mention it here. I will leave it to you to decide if this ritual is for you or not. This ritual is very optional.

The Initiation Ritual

This should be one of the first rituals you perform when you start working with The Forty Servants. This ritual has three phases. In the first phase you make contact with The Saint over a three day period and then in the second phase you ask him to introduce you to the other remaining thirty nine Servants. In the final phase you spend a further three days thanking The Saint for his help and assistance.

Think of The Saint as being similar to Scirlin from The True Grimoire, or any of the other intermediary spirits from any grimoire or system. The Saint, in this first early role, is the Servant who works as intermediary between the new magician and the Forty Servants.

Take The Saint card out of the deck, or use his sigil or printed image, and place him on your altar, or in a special place for three days. Each day, light a new candle and burn incense in his honour. Rum is also an excellent offering. Then say the following out loud to him:

I call on you Great Servant THE SAINT to come to me so I may know you.
*I am **(say your name)**, the master and ruler of this domain.*
You are the servant known for intercession and calling on experts,

come forth and introduce yourself to me.

*Ever obey me, Great Servant and ever please me.
In return I will offer you acknowledgement and sustenance
so that your energy, potency and fame increase.*

*Give me a sign that you have heard my call and
have come forth to welcome me as your Master and Friend.*

On the fourth day and for the next thirty nine days use the following prayer, changing it each day to include the name of each of the remaining thirty nine Servants in alphabetical order. Make an offering to both The Saint and the Servant on each day.

*I call on you Great Servant The Saint to come to me so I may know you.
I am **(say your name)**, the master and ruler of this domain.
I call you here so that you can introduce me to the Servant _____,
who is known for_____,*

*Oh great Servant The Saint,
bring (**The Servant's name**) forth so that I may recognise **him/her/it**,
And in return **he/she/it** will recognise me
as **his/her/their** friend and master.*

Ever obey me, Great Servant (Name of the Servant of the day) and ever please me.

In return I will offer you acknowledgement and sustenance so that your energy, potency and fame increase.

Give me a sign that you have heard my call and have come forth to welcome me as your Master and Friend.

I make these offerings as a thanks to both of you.

After concluding the introductions to each of the Servants place The Saint on your altar, or in a special place for three days. Each day make an offering and thank him in your own words for his help.

If you are wondering if this Initiation ritual is mandatory then my answer is that it is just a suggestion. As always, go with whatever feels best to you, but with that said, I would try to make sure that you aren't just avoiding doing the ritual due to impatience, or laziness.

From here you have a number of options on how you can use The Forty Servants for magick or divination:

Offerings

There are a number of ways that you can incorporate these servitors into your magick.

The simplest method is to pick a card that you feel will help you solve the problem you are experiencing. Then place it somewhere that no one else will see or disturb it (or on your altar if you have one). Light a candle in front of it and ask for the servitor's help. Speak to it like you would speak to anyone else, as if they are right there in front of you. Lighting incense can also be helpful.

Novenas

For bigger workings you can do a novena where you light a fresh candle daily for nine days and speak your wishes out loud to the card, as a prayer or just a statement of desire. A public thank you is sometimes offered as "payment" after the desired outcome has been achieved (never give the thanks offering before then), but this isn't mandatory. Find your own way to thank them, but do thank them.

Invoking

This method involves identifying with the Servant and letting the energy come into your body or mind or personality, depending on the desired result. This is probably best explained with an example.

Say you have a public talk to give and it terrifies you. You could pick a card like The Master and invoke him into you. The Master represents the you that you will become when you have all your issues sorted out and when you have become the perfect person you want to be. This perfected person would have no problems talking to people, so for the time of the event you can borrow this energy and wear it as your own.

To invoke, simply see the energy of the Servant

come into your body. Try to feel as best you can what it would feel like to be that energy or person. How would that person walk, talk or act? This takes a bit of practice but is quite effective once you get the hang of it. You can also visualize the Servant's sigil entering your body and filling you up with its energy. Drawing the sigil on your body or keeping it on your person can also be very helpful.

Binding and Banishing

Binding, in this case, is when you want to have something bound or attached to you, such as **good fortune** (The Fortunate), **creativity** (The Idea) or **sexual prowess** (The Carnal). To do this you can use the sigil from the card and draw it on your body or on something (like a stone or paper) and carry it with you as a talisman.

You can also draw the sigils in the air (either with your mind or you finger) if you need to use them when you don't have the deck at hand. An example would be to draw The Protector sigil in the air if you are in a situation that makes you feel threatened or scared.

You can also bind servitors to other people, but doing this without their permission is sometimes considered bad form or if severe enough - **black magick**! I'll leave it up to you to decide on this area. Who am I to tell you what your boundaries should be?

To bind other people, use the same techniques above, with the easiest method being to visualise the respective sigil entering their body. This is great for sending **healing** (The Healer) or sending **good luck** (The Fortunate), or even to **curse** someone (The Depleted or The Desperate).

Banishing is when you want to get rid of something. Need to cut ties with a lover? Then you could draw the sigil of The Lovers on a stone and throw it into a lake while stating your intent and desire to be free. If you have someone who is giving you a hard time at work, you could use the sigil of The Opposer. Write it on a piece of paper and burn it, throw it in the trash or walk to the edge of your town and leave it there without looking back. You could also write the name of the person on paper, add the sigil of the desired card and then put it in your freezer to chill out.

There are plenty of ways to do these things, but the most effective methods will be the ones that you come up with yourself and feel powerful to you.

If you want to know more about banishing then you can check out my blog where I have a detailed post about it:
http://bit.ly/Woobanishing

Mantras

Each Servant has a mantra that you can repeat to increase that particular Servant's energy in your life. You can use Japa beads to aid you in counting your mantras. Japa beads traditionally have 108 beads on them, and you would move from one bead to the next saying the mantra as you touch each one.

Prayers

Each Servant has a prayer that can be recited to help increase the energy of that Servant in your life. The prayers ask the Servants to teach us how to be more like them.

Map Magick

This arrived as a suggestion in the Forty Servants Facebook group from Josh Horton and I loved the idea immediately. Basically you find your house on a map such as Google Maps and print out both the house and a part of the surrounding area to give it context. Then you draw sigils over your house for whatever energy or influence you would like to bring in. For instance you could place The Protector's sigil on the house for general protection, or use The Fortunate's sigil to attract good luck and happiness into the house. You could even place sigils in individual rooms by drawing out your house layout or better still if you have the original house plans.

This technique, of course, lends itself very well to curse or baneful work where you would place sigils over an enemy's house, a place of work, or even an institution.

Spirits of Place

The Saint, The Witch and The Dead are excellent Servant choices to use to be introduced to the spirits of a new home, your area or community, a location you have or will be travelling to, or anywhere that you would like to get to know the local energies. Simply place one or all three images on your altar or special place and ask in your own words that you be introduced to and made aware of any local spirits, entities or energies. Then make offerings to both the Servants and the local spirits.

Spring and Autumn Rituals

The **Spring Ritual** is for personal renewal and a return to feeling beautiful, sexy and attractive. The **Autumn Ritual** is for releasing all the stuff that holds you back so new growth can begin. People all over the world will be doing this ritual at the same time as you, so you can tap into this group energy to amplify your own working. Obviously Spring and Autumn occur at opposite times in different hemispheres so if you use the group connection be aware that not everyone will be working the same ritual as you. This won't be a problem as everyone will still get the benefit of the group interaction and combined energy no matter what ritual they are performing.

THE RITUAL

1. Find a quiet place where you can perform the ritual without being disturbed. Switch off phones and anything that beeps for attention.
2. Take several big breaths – in through the nose and out through the mouth. Feel your lungs fill first from the bottom, then the middle and then the top of the chest.
3. Return to your normal breathing pattern.

4. If you have a banishing ritual you normally perform do that now, if not then you can clear the working area by repeating "*Hekas, Hekas Este Bebeloi*" ("Afar, Afar, O ye Profane!") while turning in an anti-clockwise direction pushing any "bad stuff" for miles in every direction using the back of your right hand. You can also burn incense such as sage or Palo Santo.
5. If you want to connect with other people doing this ritual then get out **The Unifying Sigil** and ask that you be connected to the rest of the group performing this ritual, then ask that the door to the shared sacred space that is to be used is opened to you. Try to feel a connection to the rest of the group. This can be a visualization, or just a feeling or general sense that you are connected and working together.
6. Lay out the entire deck in front of you (if you have room) or just have them in front of you in the box (Facing North is good, but not always possible)
7. Perform the steps outlined below for whatever ritual you are doing and once completed return to this section.
8. Add any personal petitions or desires you have and include any other servants you want to include at this point. You don't have to do this, just if you want to.
9. Light candles, incense or give any offerings you want in any style you choose, to the entire deck of Servants.

10. Thank the Servants, thank the rest of the group, and either then return your deck to where you normally keep it or place it on the altar or somewhere you feel is auspicious.
11. To close clap your hands once loudly having the intention to mark the end of the working. Say "And it is done" or something that feels correct to you. Or if you have you own favorite closing technique just do whatever you normally would.
12. Take photos or leave some feedback in the Facebook group so the rest of us can get to see/hear how it went for you.

SPRINGTIME – RENEWAL AND FEELING SEXY!

1. Have The Carnal image and sigil before you. Ask for the energy of The Carnal to come into your body – feel as sexy, beautiful and attractive as you can possibly let yourself be.
2. Sit with this feeling for as long as possible. Then ask The Carnal to help renew and restore your feelings of self-worth, attractiveness and sexiness!
3. Ask for inspiration in the most relevant area of your life. Ask that when inspiration comes, it does so with all the power of the

Spring and excitement of new growth and renewal.
4. Ask for clarity and guidance on how to maintain this wonderful feelings of self-love and appreciation.
5. Make an offering of candles, wine and tobacco or whatever you feel is most suitable and acceptable to The Carnal. Be creative.
6. Spend time expressing gratitude to The Carnal for her excellent work.

AUTUMN – LETTING GO AND CLEARING OUT

1. Have The Depleted image and sigil before you. Ask The Depleted to show you the parts of your life that you can let go of, that are holding you back, and that are no longer needed.
2. Feel the energy of The Depleted as it enters your body and removes all the etheric junk, emotional baggage and all the dark stuff that you no longer need. Feel this in all your bodies – physical, mental, etheric, emotional, etc.
3. Ask for inspiration and guidance of how best to clear your life of unneeded stuff so that you can start to grow again from a

better foundation. Ask that when inspiration comes, it does so with all the power of the Autumn and the great feeling of letting go and clearing out.
4. Ask for the clarity and guidance on how to proceed in your life goals.
5. Make an offering of candles, wine and tobacco or whatever you feel is suitable. A good offering here would be to clear out an old drawer or wardrobe or something like that. Be creative.
6. Spend time expressing gratitude to The Depleted for his excellent work.

The Forty Day Ritual

This Ritual is quite similar to the Initiation Ritual but doesn't involve asking The Saint to introduce you to the Servants. Instead this ritual can be used at any time to work with all the Servants on bigger magickal workings or goals. Use it when you feel your magick practice needs a super charge. This working must be done in a strict unbroken forty continuous days – one Servant a day. If you miss a day you have to start again from the first Servant.

Starting with The Adventurer and going through the Servants alphabetically you will pick out one card a day and place it on your altar (or somewhere that feels powerful to you). Light a tea light candle as an offering and say the following (out loud if possible):

I call on you Great Servant _____ to come to me.
I am ____, the master and ruler of this domain.
You are the servant known for ____*,
Come forth and be present with me.

I call you here to help me_____**
In return I will offer you acknowledgement and sustenance
so that your energy and fame increase.

Give me a sign that you have heard my call.

*List qualities and attributes of the individual servant as you see them.
** Add your intention, goal, desire or wish at this point.

THE FORTY SERVANTS

The Adventurer

This Servant shows us how to have adventure and excitement. She encourages us to break out of our comfort zones by trying new things out there in the physical world.

This Servant represents doing new things. Travelling to new places, joining in new activities and doing exciting new things. It represents the need or desire to extend yourself and have new adventures out in the physical world.

Are you feeling bored with your life or in a rut? Does nothing ever change for you? Are you having the same conversations with the same people about the same topics? Do you long for excitement and adventure and a release from the boring prison of mundane life?

It is easy to forget that human lives are predominately lived in the small bubbles of family, places of work or social groups and you must remind yourself that there is a huge world out there external from you that you can explore.

When this Servant appears it shows you have a need for something new and wonderful to happen in your life. You have become stuck in a rut and life has become boring and stale. Plan an exciting trip, do something you normally wouldn't do, or become more spontaneous - adventure awaits! Break out of your well-worn patterns and push yourself out of your comfort zone.

It can also denote travel, journeys, parties, and exciting occasions.

You can invoke the help of The Adventurer when you need some excitement or adventure in your life. This is a great Servant to use if you are feeling bored and want something exciting to happen. But you should be careful what you wish for- interesting and exciting times often come with new challenges.

Banish this Servant if life (or a person) is getting too exciting or too high energy, or is getting out of control - an overload of The Adventurer energy can lead some to become quite mercurial in nature and have an inability to sit still or relax.

Can also be used to make sure parties and gatherings, holidays or outings are fun, exciting and successful.

MANTRA: *Life is an adventure.*

KEY WORDS:

Adventure, Excitement, Accelerate, Astound, Energize, Intensify, Going Out, Rouse, Amaze, Provoke Change, Motivate, Enliven.

THE ADVENTURER PRAYER:
Oh, great Servant The Adventurer,
who is famed for her power to excite,
I call on you to come to my aid in order to break me
out of the rut that I currently find myself stuck in.
May my life be an Adventure.

The Balancer

This Servant shows us how to keep our lives balanced and in harmony. She encourages us to keep all areas of our lives in equal proportion.

When this Servant appears she tells you that there is a need for restoring some form of balance in your life.

Are you spending too much time at work and not enough with your family or having fun? Maybe you are spending too much time on frivolous stuff and not enough time following your passions. Maybe you feel that you have been given too big a share of the workload or responsibilities? Are your finances getting out of control? Are you spending way more than you earn, or even hoarding what you are earning? Now is the time to sort that out before it becomes too late and it wears you down.

If your life is out of balance in any respect, now is the time to bring harmony to it.

You can invoke the energy of The Balancer when you need to restore order or balance in your relationships, work life, or financial matters. Also useful in business matters to keep a healthy balance between expenditure and income.

The Balancer is very helpful in restoring an equal footing in relationships when you feel someone has gotten the upper hand over you. Asking for The Balancer to even out the playing field can be quite effective.

MANTRA: *All things return to an even keel.*

KEY WORDS:
Balance, Harmony, Evenness, Symmetry, Match, Attune, Collate, Stabilize, Readjust.

THE BALANCER PRAYER:
Oh, great Servant The Balancer,
who is famed for her power to restore equilibrium,
I call on you to come to my aid in order to force the events that surround me into a more balanced and harmonious condition.
May all things be in balance.

The Carnal

This Servant shows us how to feel positive about our sexuality and physical bodies. She encourages us to feel sexy, attractive and physically desired.

This Servant is all about sexual attraction and pure base animal desires. She can indicate a need to explore or indulge in sexual impulses or desires.

Do you feel sexy and desirable, or do you feel ugly and unwanted? When The Carnal appears she suggests that now is the time for you to start feeling good about yourself and your physical needs and wants.

The Carnal reminds us that our sexual needs are important to our well-being and happiness and that we shouldn't be ashamed of them, or ever try to repress them. The Carnal suggests that you should start to express your sexuality in the manner you have always wanted to. She says you should allow yourself to feel sexy, desired and passionate.

This Servant is not about love, it is purely about the physical aspects of sex, physicality and desire.

Invoke the help of The Carnal when you feel the need to feel sexy, passionate and beautiful. She is eager to assist in improving sexual confidence. You should invoke The Carnal to feel the confidence and charisma of this Servant when you are out to impress. You will start to notice people noticing you in a new light.

You can ask The Carnal to assist you in becoming a great lover who is desired by all and leaves their lovers wanting more. The Carnal is very useful in aiding the end of a sexual drought or for putting the passion back into a stale relationship. If you are looking for a lusty relationship or a quick fling then The Carnal can help get you what you need.

The Carnal works best when used for general attraction rather than for a specific person.

MANTRA: *I am desired and lusted after.*

KEY WORDS:
Desire, Beauty, Passion, Sexiness, Lust, Self-love, Physicality, Sex, Charisma, Confidence.

THE CARNAL PRAYER:
Oh, great Servant The Carnal,
who is famed for her power to make passion known ,
I call on you to rekindle my inner lustful fire.
Let me turn heads.

The Chaste

This Servant shows us that discipline and purity are also important elements of our lives. She encourages us to refrain from sexual desire and base physical pleasures and instead concentrate on a more purified existence.

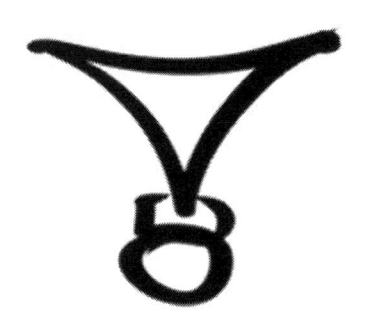

This Servant is all about refraining from the base pleasures of life and instead focusing on less physical orientated goals such as virtue, honour, purity and morality. She calls to tell you to concentrate on other areas of your life not just love, sex or physical desires.

Although at first glance it may seem like this Servant calls for restriction or a need to stop having fun, really The Chaste is suggesting that having some discipline or self-control is important to maintaining an overall healthy lifestyle, and becoming a more well-rounded person.

When this Servant appears she is saying that maybe you should spend less time focusing on your physical wants and desires and instead look inward and start developing other parts of your life - such as friendships, family, self-development or even the overall bigger picture of your life direction and goals. Is there a need to pull back and concentrate on more virtuous matters?

Perhaps you are spending too much time pursuing sexual gratification and not enough time developing other areas of your life. Has life become all about the next sexual experience? If so, The Chaste suggests now is the time to reevaluate your priorities.

The Chaste isn't always a sign encouraging physical abstinence though; she can point to the need to lessen any pursuit that you are focusing on to the detriment of other areas of your life.

You can invoke the energy of The Chaste if you are trying to pull back from a hedonistic lifestyle and want to move into a more restrained section of your life.

The Chaste is also helpful in reducing the advances of unwanted amorous admirers, or sexual partners whose sex drive is more than you want or can handle.

The Chaste can assist in all matters where purity is needed, including purity of mind. If you find yourself attracted to someone that you really shouldn't be, such as a friend's partner, then The Chaste can be asked to assist you in to purifying and releasing this harmful attraction.

MANTRA: *An end to vice and a beginning to virtue.*

KEY WORDS:
Purity, Chastity, Cleanliness, Virtue, Honour, Virginity, Innocence, Spotlessness, Faith, Goodness, Respectability, Celibacy, Abstention.

THE CHASTE PRAYER:
Oh, great Servant The Chaste,
who is famed for her power to keep people pure and virtuous,
I ask that you teach me to focus away from my vices,
so that I can be pure, clean and chaste.
May I become a virtuous person.

The Conductor

This Servant shows us how to take control of our life circumstances. He encourages us to take a more active role in orchestrating and arranging the events of our lives.

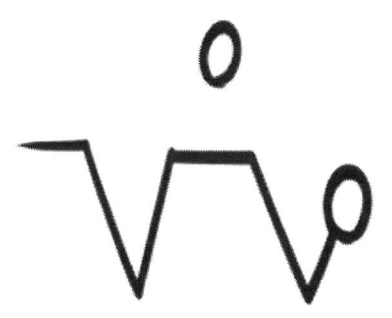

The Conductor is the magician of the orchestra, using his wand to control the music and rhythm to his preference. He is all about taking control and being in charge of the world around you. Are you the conductor leading the orchestra or are you one of the minor players? Are you being swayed in time with the music that's being played or are you marching to the beat of your own drum?

This Servant suggests that you take a look at the circumstances of your life and see what roles you are actually playing. Are you just reacting to life and accepting all that comes your way, or are you taking the lead role and living your life the way you want it to be?

Are you in flow with the music and rhythm of life and the world, or are you out of step with the beat? Is the soundtrack to your life an upbeat triumphant chorus of angels or a lonely solo violin weeping mournfully in the rain?

The Conductor calls to you to take more control over your life and to direct the music of this existence to what you want rather than just marching along to the beat of others. While you may never be fully in control of every event that occurs to or around you, you can compose your own life soundtrack to be more individual, beautiful and inspiring.

The Conductor can help you take control of events, relationships, jobs, circumstances or anything that surrounds you and put your own stamp on it.

The Conductor can show you how to move and manipulate the events of your life so that they become more harmonious and pleasing to you. The Conductor is a wonderful Servant to enlist when you feel that you don't have control or autonomy. Request The Conductor to teach you how to weave the music of life to your liking and rhythm.

MANTRA: *I am in control. I am King /Queen.*

KEY WORDS:
Control, Regulate, Order, Steer, Pilot, Rule, Authority, Domination, Manipulate, Autonomy, Self-determination, Self-rule, Sovereignty, Liberty.

THE CONDUCTOR PRAYER:
Oh, great Servant The Conductor,
who is famed for his autonomy and sovereignty,
I ask that you teach me how to orchestrate and
compose the events of my life to my liking,
so that I can be the King / Queen of my own path.
May I have control of my life.

The Contemplator

This Servant shows us how to access our subconscious mind. He encourages us to temporarily let go of thinking about our problems so that the subconscious mind can find a solution.

The Contemplator suggests that best course of action is to pull back and withdraw from thinking about your current issue for a period of time. Some problems are best solved by taking a break from thinking about them altogether or sleeping overnight on them. It's usually when we relax that the solution appears.

The Contemplator suggests that you turn your concern over to your subconscious mind to solve for you. Let the quandary fall to the back of your mind, thus allowing the subconscious to find a resolution.

This Servant can also suggest that something is buried deep within your subconscious mind and that you need to become aware of it. It could be an old idea, a limiting belief, or a bad past experience, but whatever it is, it is tainting your judgment of your current predicament.

The Contemplator has access to all the information in your subconscious mind. He is aware of all your inner workings, motivations, beliefs and long forgotten memories. He knows the underlying reasons why you do the things you do and don't do. He knows everything you have done that you weren't paying attention to. He knows more about you than you do. And you can ask him to supply you with any of this information.

Any problem can be handed over to The Contemplator for deep processing and a solution found. Visualise yourself psychically handing the issue over to The Contemplator, then try as much as possible to put it out of your mind altogether. Within the next few hours, or maybe days, the solution will suddenly appear fully formed in your mind.

The Contemplator can be asked to reveal a solution to any problem at hand. Give as full an explanation as possible regarding the nature of the problem and any pertinent information to The Contemplator. This should be spoken out loud.

In another very humble, but highly effective role, The Contemplator can help you remember details that are temporarily forgotten, such as phone numbers, people's names, or where you left your keys. Take a brief moment and mentally give the problem to The Contemplator and wait for the reply. It shouldn't be forced or pressured.

The Contemplator is also very useful for transferring new skills or information into our long-term subconscious minds for later retrieval or automation. Great for forming new habits or breaking old ones.

MANTRA: *Everything is known to me.*

KEY WORDS:
Subconscious, Information, Automation, Withdraw, Letting Solutions Present Themselves, Revelation, Subliminal.

THE CONTEMPLATOR PRAYER:
Oh, great Servant The Contemplator,
who is famed for his memory and problem solving,
reveal to me the true nature of my problem,
show what is hidden from me but known by you,
show me what I am blind to, but can be seen by you.
May the mystery be revealed.

The Dancer

This Servant shows us that it is perfectly human to fail or come up short. She encourages us to accept that sometimes things just don't work out as planned and that's perfectly fine.

When this Servant appears it is a signal that sometimes the best thing you can do when it rains is to go dance in it. Life can be hard and sometimes things just don't go the way we wanted them to no matter how hard we try. It is an inevitable part of life that sometimes, despite our finest efforts, we just lose.

And that's ok. The Dancer, however, is here to remind you that it's not ok to just give up.

The Dancer suggests that rather than spiraling into depression or becoming disheartened that you should rejoice in the effort made, and dance in the rain. Life may be falling apart around you but The Dancer reminds you that you are fully in control of your reactions towards it. You can choose to fall apart or you can choose to laugh along with it.

The Dancer reminds you that even a failure can be celebrated as it brings with it the lessons that will get you closer to your goals. When life is tough, The Dancer calls out to take things less seriously and just enjoy the moment, no matter what that moment is.

Ask The Dancer to help you stay afloat when times are tough or when your plans have failed. Invoke The Dancer when you need to pick yourself up and get back into the game.

Ask The Dancer to help you see the good even in the darkest moments or to show you the prettiness of the rain, and the joy of the dance. Let The Dancer show you how to never give up.

MANTRA: *The way things are, is the way things are.*

KEY WORDS:
Acceptance, Non-resistance, Recognition of How It Is, Being Ok, Surrender, Being a Good Loser, Surviving.

THE DANCER PRAYER:
Oh, great Servant The Dancer,
who is famed for her wonderful perspective,
teach me how to dance in the rain as you do,
so that I can accept what I have lost.
May I live to fight another day.

The Dead

This Servant shows us our connection to our Ancestors, and humanity's past. She encourages us to learn from the past, so that we don't make the same mistakes over and over.

This Servant is all about the lessons learned from history – your own personal history and our collective human history. The Dead suggests that you should heed the lessons, warnings, and advice from those who have gone before you. She reminds you that there is a huge amount of wisdom available to you from the experiences of the entire population of the world, including all who have long since died.

The Dead asks you to reflect on your past experiences so that you don't make the same mistakes again. For instance, are you making the same mistakes in this relationship as your previous ones? Are you ignoring the experiences of those who have gone before you and think that you know better? Are you dismissing an old fashioned idea or method simply because it is old? Are you ignoring messages and teachings of deceased friends, relatives or people of note?

The Dead can be used for general ancestor work. An offering to The Dead is an offering to your ancestors and the Mighty Dead and you should thank them for all they have done. Remember, you would not exist if it weren't for all those who came before you.

If someone close to you passes, you can ask The Dead to help bring them safely to the other side and to look after them as they make their way into the next stage of their existence.

You can ask The Dead to carry any messages to the deceased.

The Dead Servant can also be used to connect to any part of the past, such as family history, personal history or even the history of the area you live in.

The Dead is an exceptional Servant to use for emotional healing. If there are parts of your past that need healing you can ask The Dead to assist you to send love or comfort to a time in your life when you needed it most. The Dead can help to reconnect with parts of you that you thought were long gone or even dead.

Old hatreds or arguments with dead friends or relatives can be appeased or mended by using The Dead Servant as a conduit between the parties.

The Dead can be asked for general guidance on all matters. She is hugely knowledgeable as she has access to the entire history of human thought and deed.

MANTRA: *Though it may seem to be lost, nothing is ever truly gone.*

KEY WORDS:
Death, Ancestors, History, The Past, Antiquity, Legacy, Connection, Collective Experience, The Veil, Psychopomp, Combined Knowledge, Endings, New Phases.

THE DEAD PRAYER:
Oh, great Servant The Dead,
who is famed for her ability to connect through time and space,
show me how to learn from the past,
so that I no longer repeat my mistakes.
May I move forward not backwards.

The Depleted

This Servant shows us that all our resources have been used up in one area of our lives. It encourages us to take the time we need to replenish our stores and perhaps move in a new direction.

When this Servant appears it usually means that you have run out of energy, money, supplies, or resources and that you should stop and rest before any permanent damage is done. You have put all you can into a particular situation and have become burnt out. All power, energy, and will to continue has been drained from you.

The Depleted suggests that the only solution is to retreat and restock, regrow and allow the cycles of life to move onto the next, hopefully more rewarding stage. Winter has come and all growth has ceased. The days are dark and the nights long and no amount of renewed effort can change that.

Something in your life has run its course and needs to be allowed to end. All things naturally have an end point and it can be sometimes hard to let things go, but we must let them go if we are to continue to grow instead of withering away and dying.

What are you not letting go of? What are you holding on to that has ceased to be of value? Is there a situation that saps all your energy or time that needs to be put to bed for good? Has a relationship gone on so long that now there is nothing of value in it for anyone? Time to let the dying things die, so that new things can grow.

The Depleted can be used to remove energy from any situation you no longer want to experience. This, of course, lends itself easily to any sort of curse work- you can instruct The Depleted to drain the energy stores or resources of an enemy.

While The Depleted can be used to put an end to any situation, relationship or endeavor, it must be noted that in cases of attack magick, the depletion can spread out wider than just the target. Everyone's life affects the people and events around them, so draining energy from a single person or circumstance will have knock on effects on the surrounding events and lives. This is unavoidable and as such should always be a consideration.

The Depleted can be used safely in personal matters to easily end things that have come to their natural conclusion but just refuse to complete cease such as lingering legal matters, or ex's that just won't move on.

MANTRA: *All must end, for the new to begin.*

KEY WORDS:
Endings, Cycles, Drained, Emptied, Sapped, Spent,

Used Up, Finished, Over, Worn Out, Seasons,
Weary, Withered, Complete.

THE DEPLETED PRAYER:
Oh, great Servant The Depleted,
who shows us that the time has come for things to end,
please teach me how to let this need of mine go,
may all the old things be replaced with the new.
May freshness replace the tired and worn out.

The Desperate

This Servant shows us that everything is currently as bad as it can get. He encourages us to recognise the hell we are in.

If you are looking for the most negative Servant, then The Desperate is it. When this Servant appears it is a sign that you are going through an intense period of depression, sadness or hopelessness. Things feel about as bad as they possibly can be and no end seems to be in sight.

You are feeling frustrated, angry, and hopeless- all at the same time. Nothing matters, no one cares, nothing ever works out, everything is pointless, and only the end of physical life seems like an escape – and even that isn't a guarantee, as who knows if death is actually any better?

You have found yourself in a hole that you probably won't be able to get out of by yourself. This is crisis time and it must be taken seriously by those around you.

The Desperate suggests that unless you makes

big changes in the direction you are headed the future may become, or remain, quite bleak.

The Desperate is a Servant of emotional inner turmoil. Your outward life circumstance may not appear to a causal onlooker to be anything that bad- it might even look good- but inside your head you are in hell, and there is no escape.

The upside to this is that events can't get any worse. This is as low and terrible as it gets. Life is cyclical and nothing last forever. When you get to the other side of this initiation you will be all the better for it, and will a much stronger person.

The function of The Desperate is to be in desperation. This is what he knows, this is all he experiences. You can give him all your desperation, suffering, torment and pain. Give him all your misery, anguish, sorrow and sadness, and let him take it from you and use it to sustain himself. Let The Desperate take on the burden of your hardships, for hardship is all that he knows.

Love and healing can be sent to The Desperate as an embodiment of all the pain and suffering in the world and throughout history. Offerings made to The Desperate will aid all those enduring suffering and hardship.

The Desperate can be banished; you can place the sigil on a stone and throw it into the sea, or write the sigil on paper and burn or bury it.

Like The Depleted Servant, The Desperate also lends itself easily to curse work. Sending The Desperate to torture an enemy is very effective but obviously if things go too far the responsibility will be yours. This is the worst Servant of them all, the most horrible, the most vicious and the most severe. Use only if necessary.

MANTRA: *Take from me my sorrows.*

KEY WORDS:
Dire, Terrible, Drastic, Pain, Suffering, Depression, Sadness, Torment, Misery, Dark Clouds, Hopeless, Despondent, Forlorn.

THE DESPERATE PRAYER:
Oh, great Servant The Desperate
who is demented with eternal torments,
I offer to you all my pain and suffering,
take it from me and use it as sustenance.
My worries are now yours, my pain is now yours,
my suffering is now yours, my misery is now yours.
May they torment me no longer,
As they now all belong to you.

The Devil

This Servant shows us the beliefs we hold that restrict us and keep us from true freedom. He encourages us to realise that we have placed these binds upon ourselves and can break free whenever we want.

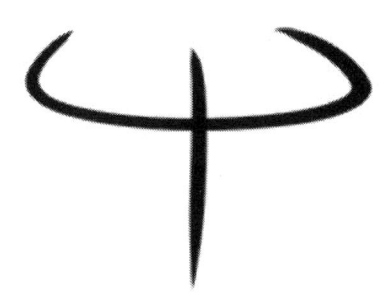

The Devil Servant knows that something you believe about life or yourself is blocking you from getting what you want. The Devil tells you that you are needlessly restricting yourself because of some rule, or "truth" you have decided to live by or believe.

When this Servant appears it is a reminder to look at what beliefs, or rules you have around your current situation or problem, and judge whether they are useful or not. The chances are that deep down you don't really believe these self-imposed rules to be true, but you follow them out of a sense of duty, or simply because you always just thought that way.

You have many rules about how you should

behave or act, what is acceptable and what isn't, and even what you are allowed to enjoy and what you shouldn't enjoy. All your life you have been told that some things are "wrong" or "sinful" but have you ever really stopped to think if you actually agree with these rules?

The Devil tells you that it is only you making up these rules- there isn't an ultimate and true morality, just your opinions on the nature of good and evil. The Devil calls for you to let go of guilt and allow yourselves to behave the way you feel is right, not the way you have may been told is right.

When you find yourself acting on a restricting belief that you no longer want, visualize The Devil's sigil pushing this belief away from your body and far away from you.

If you are unsure of what limiting beliefs you may have that are holding you back, The Devil can be asked to show you them. Events and circumstances will appear in your life such that these beliefs and rules come to the surface for you to observe. Once you recognise them you can begin to work past them and then release them.

In attack magick, the Devil can be used to bind someone to continue deeper and deeper in their own folly. If you observe that an opponent is doing harm to you, or something you are involved with, due to their personal beliefs and rules, you can send The Devil to push them further into this limiting mindset, bringing it front and center in their lives. This usually leads to the target fully overcoming their need for these restrictions and seeing their folly. But sometimes they become totally engulfed and further immersed in their belief systems, destroying themselves in the process.

MANTRA: *The chains that bind me are now broken.*

KEY WORDS:
Restriction, Limitation, Bounds, Binds, Confinement, Blocks, Constraint, Impediment, Inhibition, Taboo.

THE DEVIL PRAYER:
Oh, great Servant The Devil
who gives knowledge of how we needlessly restrict ourselves,
show me the chains that I bind myself with,
so that I may break free from them.
May I no longer hold myself back.

The Explorer

This Servant shows us how to become a better person by exploring the depths of ourselves. He encourages us to be more committed to our personal development and to find our hidden talents and potential.

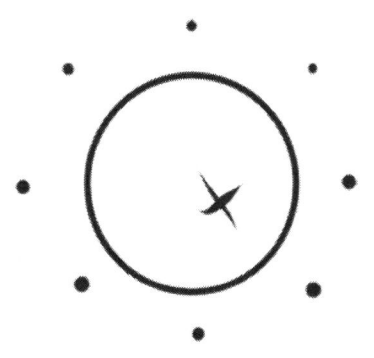

This Servant is all about self-growth and exploration, personal development, and becoming a better version of who you are. It's time for you to start breaking out of your personal comfort zones and explore new ideas, passions and talents.

The Explorer signals a period of learning and self-discovery that while sometimes painful to experience (all growth is somewhat painful as the old must die for the new to live), the end result will always be that you are a much better, happier, confident and more content person.

The Explorer is the Servant of personal development and self-help. He suggests that you should do a new personal development course, read some self-help books, take up yoga or begin a meditation practice. If you already do these things, then The Explorer tells you to up your game or move into new areas of development.

The Explorer is a call to realise that you can be much more than you currently are letting yourself be. It's time to widen yourself, push yourself and see just what you are capable of.

He also shows up to remind you about skills, talents or goals you may have forgotten about. Have you always wanted to paint, write, start gardening, compose music, or similar but have never gotten round to it? The Explorer suggests that now is the time to start working on developing these skills before they are lost to time forever.

The Explorer says to set bigger goals, learn new skills, overcome limiting beliefs and go explore more about who you really are. Rekindle or find the brilliance and potential you have within. Strive to become a much better and greater version of yourself.

The Explorer can be invoked to help with any personal development related tasks or desires. The Explorer can help you discover talents or abilities you aren't aware you possess.

He can teach you the skills and knowledge you need to become a stronger and better person

Invoking The Explorer will show the operator just how big they and their world actually are, and how to make themselves even bigger, wider, more powerful and more complete. The Explorer will help them become the person they are ultimately to become.

MANTRA: *Who I am is limitless.*

KEY WORDS:
Personal Development, Self-Help, Inner Exploration, Setting New Challenges, Goal Setting.

THE EXPLORER PRAYER:
Oh, great Servant The Explorer
who calls for us to widen our personal horizons,
show me I can progress and move forward,
so that I may become more complete and whole.
May I always be improving.

The Eye

This Servant shows us that there is a Divine plan to all things. It encourages us to remember that all is as it should be.

When The Eye appears it is a sign that all is going according to plan, even if it doesn't appear so from your perspective. The catch is that the plan that is on track is *the Divine plan*, which may not be what you had in mind.

The advice given by this Servant is that even if life appears to be going all wrong or falling apart - it will all work out for the best in the end. You will eventually end up in the place you are meant to be in and when you look back you will see how every moment had to occur exactly as it did to allow everything to fall into place.

The Eye is also a sign that someone or something from the spirit realm is looking out for you, and that you are being looked after and helped, even if you don't feel it. Ultimately, The Eye is a reminder of the existence of a higher being or beings watching over us, guiding and helping us from a far.

The Eye is your connection to the Super Consciousness, of which your own consciousness is just a microcosm, or aspect. Invoking The Eye will infuse you with Spirit and Divine Presence. This Presence is the original thought that existed at the beginning of all things and will be there at the very end - it is consciousness in the fullest and widest sense. It is all things. It can take many shapes or forms, and will present itself differently to every person.

The Eye can be used to help you become more in-sync with the higher calling of life. The Eye can be the focus of prayers for the safety, healing and happiness of all sentient beings in the universe.

MANTRA: *All is as it should be.*

KEY WORDS:
Faith, Divine Plan, On Track, Protection, Help from Above, Spirit, Presence, Guidance.

THE EYE PRAYER:
Oh, great Servant The Eye
who knows the great plan of existence,
show me how to stay on the right track,
so that I live in harmony with all creation.
May all beings be without suffering.

The Father

This Servant shows us tough love, guidance, and wisdom so that we can face the challenges of life for ourselves. He encourages us to learn the lessons for ourselves so that we handle future problems with greater wisdom and insight.

When The Father appears it means that someone in your life will offer guidance and wisdom on how to deal with your current issue or problem. However, it may be that you need to seek out such a person if none is at hand.

This Servant tells you that it is ok to look for help, guidance or to rely on the wisdom of other more experienced people. Someday you may know all the answers but for the time being it is wiser to ask someone who will be able to steer you on the right path.

The Father loves you, his child, and only wants the best for you, but he knows that sometimes tough love may be the best solution. The Father card tells you that you may be about to hear or be obliged to do something you don't like, but that ultimately it is the correct and wise thing to do.

The Father is full of love and will offer all the wisdom and insight that he has at his disposal. However he wants you to be able to fend for yourself, with his ultimate goal being that you are able to navigate this world on your own. He believes that the best way for you to learn something is by doing it or experiencing it for yourself.

Life has hardships and problems that we all must go through, and The Father knows this. He wants you to be prepared for these, and will stand by your side giving advice and wisdom as you do. He won't protect you from these experiences as he knows the growth and strength that comes from overcoming our own battles and problems. The Father knows that the only true way of learning to not put your hand in the fire is to experience doing it once, no amount of advice can replace experience.

The Father is an exceptional Servant to use when you need guidance on a big life decisions such as: should I switch jobs? Is now a good time to sell? What is the best way to deal with this issue or person? How do I learn to live without someone? Should I stay in this relationship? Is this a good investment of my time or money? What's my best next move? The advice may not always be what you want to hear but deep down you will know it is the right move.

A great Servant for any time when guidance, advice or wisdom is needed on real life issues.

MANTRA: *I am not alone.*

KEY WORDS:
Guidance, Wisdom, Learning from Experience, Fending for Yourself, Practical Advice.

THE FATHER PRAYER:
Oh, great Servant The Father
who gives great counsel on the ways of life,
tell me what my best option is
so that I can make the wisest move.
May I heed your insights so that I avoid unneeded pain.

The Fixer

This Servant shows us that any problem can be solved if we are willing to do what is needed. He encourages us to do what must be done to get the desired outcome we seek – no matter the cost.

Any problem or challenge can be solved, but there is always some cost involved in the solution. The Fixer asks the question: are you willing to pay the price for what you want? You can get whatever it is that you desire but you will have to accept all the costs that go with it.

Paying the price, however, doesn't always mean something terrible. The cost of writing a book, for instance, is the long months or years sitting on your own writing. You must deal with the frustrations and the pain that go with writing. For some people that pain is totally worth it, for others it really isn't. The Fixer wants you to think about the costs involved in the resolution of your own situation and asks if you are willing to accept the price.

Is the resolution of the problem worth the cost or

is it better just to walk away?

The Fixer Servant is only used when all else has failed or no other option is available. He is not a Servant to engage without thinking things through fully. Are you willing to do anything to get your desired goal? Are you willing to pay whatever the cost of business is? Many times you may not know the full cost of something until it is over, and by then it is too late to change your mind, so you have to be very sure you are willing to accept whatever fallout occurs.

To set The Fixer to work, you should explain the circumstances of the problem to him, and then tell him that he should fix it. Then, and most importantly, you should say out loud that you will accept whatever the cost is by stating that you are willing to accept the ramifications of whatever it is that has to be done, or that has to occur in order for you to get your desired outcome. Once on the job he cannot be recalled until the task is complete.

You'll know what the price is when you get what you wanted as usually the two things happen at the same time. The Price and The Desire are intrinsically linked. The price you pay is not really to The Fixer, it's more about what you are OK with happening or doing in order to get what you want.

As an example: The price of getting a promotion is that the person who currently has the job has to lose it. This could mean they will get fired. It could also mean they too get a promotion. But you can't know until it happens and you have to be OK with both outcomes.

The Fixer is only to be used when you have tried

every other means. The Fixer will do "whatever it takes" so you have to be sure that's what you want. Use with extreme caution and only as a last resort.

MANTRA: *There is always a solution.*

KEY WORDS:
Solution, Adjust, Fix, Sort Out, Repair, Patch, Price to Pay, Cost, Last Resort.

THE FIXER PRAYER:
Oh, great Servant The Fixer
who find solutions to even the worst of problems,
resolve my problem by doing whatever needs to done.
I am willing to pay the price that is required.
May I learn to live with my decision.

The Fortunate

This Servant shows us how to be happy, healthy, wealthy and wise. She encourages us to recognise just how good life can be.

If The Desperate is the worst Servant to see in a reading then The Fortunate is certainly the best. When The Fortunate appears it is a sign that everything is going really great for you, or is just about to be.

The Fortunate is a herald of prosperous times- life is good, things are easy, and the future is bright. If this Servant's card is chosen as an answer to a question, then the answer is a resounding **yes!**

The Fortunate tells you that it's time to live and be happy, to be joyful and relaxed in the knowledge that everything is going perfectly. The sun is shining brightly on you, all the omens are good, and all worries are vanishing. Life is as good as it can be.

The Fortunate is very effective in all money magick workings. Asking The Fortunate for good luck and good fortune with money is usually very successful. With money magick it is traditionally suggested that you start with asking for a small amount of money rather than going for billions immediately. While everything is possible, magick works best with the probable - a pay rise is a better ask than a lottery win.

The Fortunate can also be asked for good luck in any endeavor, including exams, job interviews, opening new businesses, gambling, sports events, and even bargain hunting. You can invoke the energy of The Fortunate at any time you need to feel lucky.

For curse work you could ask The Fortunate to change the good luck of your enemy into bad luck. Being lucky works both ways, after all.

MANTRA: *Everything is wonderful.*

KEY WORDS:
Happiness, Success, Joy, Wonder, Prosperity, Riches, Opulence, Good Times, Abundance, Luxury, Plenty, Comfort, Delight, Elation.

THE FORTUNATE PRAYER:
Oh, great Servant The Fortunate
who showers the blessed with riches and happiness,
send me some good luck and good fortune,
so that I can delight in the good times.
May I live in abundance.

The Gate Keeper

This Servant shows us how to get into areas of our life that we feel locked out of. He encourages us to know that there is always a key to every door.

The Gate Keeper suggests that you feel like you are being locked out of something - a clique, a career path, an opportunity, a family secret, a group or even a physical place such as a new house. It may be just a feeling, or it may be very much the case. You can be locked out because of your own actions, the actions of others, or unavoidable life circumstances. In the reading, other cards may suggest where the fault lies, but perhaps it may already be obvious to you.

The Gate Keeper says that there is always a way to get access to what we want and it is just a matter of finding the correct procedure, or getting in contact with the right person.

This Servant can also suggest that information is being deliberately withheld from you. Someone or something is being hidden from view. Someone is keeping something secret.

The Gate Keeper holds the keys to the other side of the spiritual veil. He can give access to heaven, the underworld, the astral plane, hell, or any other spiritual plane or area that you desire to interact with, in order to communicate with those who dwell there. A spoken request of "Great Servant, The Gate Keeper, please open the door Gate Keeper, so I may pass and speak to those on the other side" with offerings of candles or incense upon your return, is very effective.

The Gate Keeper can help locate lost or stolen items as no door is closed to him, and for this reason he is also exceptional at revealing secrets or hidden things. Nothing can be hidden from The Gate Keeper. The Gate Keeper can grant you access to known places, contacts or opportunities that you are currently locked out of or somehow restricted from entering, such as jobs, new houses, social circles, cliques, or social clubs.

MANTRA: *All doors are open.*

KEY WORDS:
Access, Exposed, Revealed, Available, Permitted, Obtainable, Open Door, Accessible, Unfastened.

THE GATE KEEPER PRAYER:
Oh, great Servant The Gate Keeper
who holds the key to every lock,
open the door for me so that I may pass

and speak to those on the other side.
May I be given entrance.

The Giver

This Servant shows us all the great gifts we have received in our lives. He encourages us to remember to always be generous and grateful as today you may be the giver but tomorrow you may be the receiver.

When The Giver appears it is an indication that a gift is about to be given to you. This gift can take many forms: unexpected money, some good news, generosity from a stranger, a miracle, a heartfelt compliment from a friend, or experiencing something that touches your heart and lifts your soul.

The Giver is all about generosity and gratitude, and the giving and taking exchange. When this Servant appears in a reading it is a call for you to remember all the gifts that have been given to you, and all the generosity you have experienced in your life. It is easy to forget the goodness in people but this Servant comes to reminds us to be ever grateful for them.

The Giver is also about miracles and Divine gifts - those unexpected occurrences that seem to come from nowhere that change everything, completely remove the problem, or save us from the depths of despair. Watch out for them, as the appearance of this Servant suggests one is on its way to you.

The Giver is very useful and powerful to enlist when you are trying to make business deals or are involved in any sort of exchange or trade agreement. The Giver can be asked to ensure that the deal turns out fair for all sides, or at the very least fair for you. The Giver can be used in any working where exchanges are being made.

The Giver can be engaged to help when you need a minor miracle, but like The Fixer a price must be paid. The price in this case is that you have to return the favour to someone else. Don't over think this. Sometimes it will be obvious what you must do for someone else in return for your miracle, sometimes it won't be. Best practice is to just go out of your way to do something nice for another person without wanting or expecting anything in return.

The Giver can be helpful in cases where you have offered forgiveness but it has not been accepted. At these times ask The Giver to help smooth things over and restore the relationship.

MANTRA: *To give is to receive.*

KEY WORDS:
Award, Benefit, Charity, Present, Offering, Bestowal, Gratuity, Acceptance, Generosity, Collect, Obtain, Gift, Give and Take, Receive,

Contract, Possession.

THE GIVER PRAYER:
Oh, great Servant The Giver,
who gives all with wondrous and selfless generosity
of spirit
send me the gift of a miraculous occurrence,
so that I escape my current fate.
May all beings receive what they need.

The Guru

This Servant shows us how to apply any knowledge we have gained in a practical way. He encourages us to always try to implement the lessons learned from our spiritual insights in our day to day lives.

The Guru suggests that a new spiritual or magick mentor has entered into your life, or is very shortly about to appear. Guru is a Sanskrit term that connotes someone who is a "teacher, guide, expert, or master" of a certain knowledge or field. The Guru can take many forms so don't be too hasty in dismissing someone because of how they look or behave. Sometimes the best wisdom comes from unexpected quarters.

The Guru suggests a more one on one relationship than the typical teacher and class system, but doesn't totally rule it out. The Guru is a teacher, guide, friend, mentor and spiritual counsel. He will impart wisdom, understanding and practical advice rather than just intellectual knowledge. He will show you **how** to do things rather than why you should do them, or give you the theory behind the practice. The Guru is extremely practical.

The Guru Servant is extremely useful to invoke when you are in need of practical spiritual direction or mentoring in some area of esoterica, magick or spirituality. He is a great Magician and Spiritual Master but his emphasis is always on the practical application of magical or spiritual ideas in your day to day life.

He is also extremely useful when you need to learn any sort of new practical skill. Tell the Guru the problems you are facing, the new skill you want to learn, or the ideas or concepts you are having a challenge implementing in your life, and then ask that they be explained or revealed to you in practical and useful terms.

The Guru can be invoked during times when you find yourself being asked to give spiritual advice or counsel, but you are not sure what the best advice to give is, or you are being put on the spot and are lost for an answer. Using the sigil, you can invoke The Guru into yourself and allow his wisdom and guidance to pour through you.

MANTRA: *It's no use unless you can use it.*

KEY WORDS:

Teaching, Functional, Practical, Skills, Application of Ideas, Mentor, Spiritual Master, Pragmatic, Matter-of-Fact, Direction, Using Knowledge, Application of Ideas.

THE GURU PRAYER:
Oh, great Servant The Guru,
who is the most skillful Magician, and master of spirit,
teach me how to use my knowledge in practical ways,
so I can become a skillful and functional magician.
May my knowledge be put into practice.

The Healer

This Servant shows us how to heal and recover. She encourages us to always look after ourselves and others.

The Healer suggests that you may be in danger of getting sick or worn out. This sickness may not be physical; it can be emotional or even spiritual. The appearance of The Healer in a reading suggests that now is the time for you to start looking after yourself. Perhaps you should go get a check up with a doctor or start a healthy diet. The Healer also suggest that you should consider exercising more and becoming as physically fit and healthy as possible.

The Healer can also denote the arrival of a person in your life who will bring with them fantastic healing energy, or who will be a soothing and healing influence on you and your life. Perhaps it is someone from the past who now wants to settle old hurts, but it could just as easily be someone new to your life who just has a very curative presence.

If The Healer appears and you are currently sick, then it is a sign that you are on the road to recovery as long as you get the necessary rest and recuperation you need.

The Healer can be used for all healing work or rituals. This ranges from general "healing the world" offerings to more focused healing sent or aimed at a particular person (or event). Candle offerings work extremely well coupled with asking The Healer to look after your loved ones while they are sick. You can also ask for healing for yourself. Drawing the sigil above sick people (either physically with the hand or just visualising it with the mind) while asking for The Healer's healing and soothing presence can be beneficial.

The Healer can also be called to protect and keep safe those who work in the healing, medicine and rescue services.

Note: The Healer is in no way meant as an alternative to your doctor or conventional medical treatment. If you or the people in your care are sick or unwell, get it checked out by a professional.

MANTRA: *All is well.*

KEY WORDS:
Healing, Curative, Soothing, Rest, Mending, Recovery, Sickness, Health, Medicine, Restorative, Therapeutic, Tonic, Wholeness, Wellness, Well-Being.

THE HEALER PRAYER:
Oh, great Servant The Healer,
who is the most healing and soothing of all the Servants,
assist me in this healing miracle to occur,
so that I/she/he/they can return to full strength and health.
May all beings be well.

The Idea

This Servant shows us how to be original, inventive and creative. It encourages us to see that inspiration is always around us.

When The Idea appears it is a reminder that you have been given an idea for something that should be expanded upon and brought into existence. These ideas don't hang round for too long and if you hesitate you may find yourself looking at someone else bringing "your" idea into the world and reaping all the benefits that could have been yours.

The Idea wanders around looking for people who will take a seed and grow something big out of it. The Idea doesn't care who the person is who turns the Idea into reality, it just wants the creation to get out into the world.

The Idea urges you that now is the time to develop the ideas you have rather than letting them linger in the back of your mind to work on, or get to "someday" - that someday is now, and if you don't act soon, someone else will.

The Idea is great for any situation that needs the creative spark. The Idea is excellent for invoking at the start of a creative project or when some fresh new creative ideas are needed. You can place the sigil in your office or place of work, so that a constant flow of ideas and creativity come your way.

It is also possible to use The Idea to bind an idea to yourself so that no one else uses it. That said, some ideas are so strong that they just need to get out no matter what so it is always better to act soon rather than regret it later.

Candle offerings to The Idea can help to motivate your team/group/friends to be more creative. Generally anything to do with creativity, ideas, imagination and inspiration is The Idea's wheelhouse.

MANTRA: *Creativity is easy.*

KEY WORDS:
Creativity, Inspiration, Ideas, Imagination, Ingenuity, Originality, Vision, Design, Discover, Form, Invention, Compose, Illumination.

THE IDEA PRAYER:
Oh, great Servant The Idea,
who exudes inspiration, creativity, insight and understanding
fill my head and being with new wonderful ideas

---

so that I make them a reality in the world.
May creativity come easily to all.

The Levitator

This Servant shows us how to rise above the drama in our lives so we can stay aloof and detached. He encourages us to try to see things from a different angle.

It is easy to take life too seriously or be so rooted in a problem that it is all you can see. The Levitator suggests that you rise above it all and stop participating in the game. Will you care about any of this a month from now? A year from now? Ten years from now? The chances are that the problems that currently feel all-consuming will soon be nothing more than a memory, with their sting or bite long gone.

The Levitator may also suggest that you should become the bigger person in a problem situation, or argument, and perhaps allow the other person to win for the sake of peace. Maybe you should make the first move towards reconciliation after a falling out or argument with someone.

When The Levitator appears in a reading it is

often a suggestion for you to look at the issues at hand from a different angle. Can you try to see your issue or problem from a different angle or perspective? Try to look at it as if it was happening to someone else. What advice would you give to someone else if they came to you with this problem?

You can use The Levitator in times when you feel that life is getting to be too much to handle, or if problem after problem is mounting up and you feel like you have no escape. The Levitator can show you the situation from a higher or wider perspective, where a bigger, more complete picture is clearly seen. From this point of view you may get a better insight into the solution of your problem, or at the very least the reason why you must endure it.

If there is a need for you to be the "bigger person" in a situation, advice can be sought from The Levitator on what is the best approach to take.

If your life has become too much about other people's drama, or a situation has become toxic, invoke The Levitator to rise above it all and become unaffected by all that is occurring. Also useful when you need to take the moral high ground.

The Levitator can also be used if you are pursuing the development of the spiritual siddhis. Invoking is key to this.

MANTRA: *I rise above it all.*

KEY WORDS:
Rising Above It All, Different Perspective,

Seeing Things From a Different Angle, Escaping the Drama, Being Aloof, Detached, Above.

THE LEVITATOR PRAYER:
Oh, great Servant The Levitator,
who rises above it all and sees the greater story,
show me how I too can escape all this drama
so that the events that surround me no longer drain me.
May the bigger picture be clear to me.

The Librarian

This Servant shows us the theory behind the subjects that interest us. She encourages us to study, and ever increase our knowledge.

The Librarian is all about studying, researching and gathering information. It is about the theory and information rather than practical application. The Librarian is interested in knowing rather than doing. She can often be a sign that education and learning of some form is important to you or that it is about to play a big part in your life.

The Librarian is mostly connected to formal education, but self-learning, rather than being taught by a teacher, is not to be ruled out as a possibility. When The Librarian appears there is often a sense of the need to gain further knowledge on a subject or problem. It may be a sign that you need to research more about the problem or topic at hand, or someway get your nose into the books. Might also indicate a return to education or doing course work.

The Librarian is a great Servant to use if you are having difficulty in procuring a particular book. A candle offering made to The Librarian with the name of the book to be located written on paper underneath it, has usually terrific results. Audiobooks, PDFs, comics or any sort of media can also be asked for.

Equally, if you are looking for a certain piece of information or data, then The Librarian is a great Servant to help with tracking it down. You can ask for what you need and will subsequently have the information come to you synchronistically.

The Librarian is also very useful if you are studying or taking exams or doing a test. A series of candle offerings, or even a novena, is very effective around exam time. Her sigil can be placed in the study area so that you retain more of the information you read. The sigil placed in the exam hall, if possible, can also be hugely beneficial.

MANTRA: *Knowledge is power.*

KEY WORDS:
Theory, Books, Information, Data, Learning, Study, Documents, Book Locating, Storage of Information, Education, Know-how, Comprehension, Exams, Tests.

THE LIBRARIAN PRAYER:
Oh, great Servant The Librarian,
who has access to all the knowledge of the world,
help me on my path to gain the information I seek
so that I become much wiser and better informed.
May knowledge flow freely.

The Lovers

This Servant shows us how to love after the lust has subsided. They encourage us to connect on a deeper level with our partners so that sacred bonds are formed.

The Lovers is not about sex or lust - it is about intimacy and acceptance. It's about partnerships, trust and synergy. It's about two separate people or things joining as one. It is about union.

The Lovers recalls that moment after your lust has been satisfied and you still want the other person to be close to you. It's the relationship after the honeymoon period where the couple really fall in love as people rather than as physical lovers. The Lovers reminds you about the closeness and union that bonds great relationships.

When The Lovers appears in a reading it suggests that there is a need for partnership. The Lovers often signals business partnerships, or new significant friendships, but it also represents deepening romantic relationships.

The Lovers can be used when you are looking for a lasting relationship, it is not a Servant for those looking for quick and easy love hook-ups with no strings attached (The Carnal is a more suitable Servant for that sort of working). Instead The Lovers is used to attract a life mate or long-term relationship.

The Lovers is also great when trying to make a relationship more loving, warm or generally closer. Candles, rose incenses, or indeed roses themselves make great offerings to The Lovers.

The Lovers is very helpful when you want to move a casual relationship to the next level, or when significant changes need to be made to the dynamic of a current relationship without causing long-term or irrevocable damage.

MANTRA: *I am safe and loved.*

KEY WORDS:
Tenderness, Devotion, Appreciation, Bonds, Respect, Attachment, Beloved, Connection, Contact, Partnership, Affinity, Sentiment.

THE LOVERS PRAYER:
Oh, great Servant The Lovers,
who holds the secret of connecting hearts,
show me how to strengthen my relationships
so that my love and devotion is matched and reciprocated.
May I be loved and cherished.

The Master

This Servant shows us how to be the best version of ourselves. He encourages us to always strive to act from our highest selves rather than our lesser natures.

The Master asks: what would you do if you were the best version of yourself? How would you approach the situation at hand from the point of view of an enlightened being?

The Master is you on your very best day - it's you on the day when you are able to handle everything the world throws at you - and with style. The Master knows in every moment what the best approach is, what to say and how to react because he has seen all this before and knows how to deal with it quickly, easily and expertly.

If you were the person you want to be what would you do, say, or think? How would you behave? This mindset can be used in times when there is a need for extra strength or confidence.

You should think of the person you were five, or ten, or twenty years ago and realise how much more you know about life now than you did then. Then think about how much you would know if you lived to be a thousand years old, a million years old or until the end of all time. How would this version of you (the ideal, or master version) deal with your current situations, goals, worries or relationships? What would the perfected version of you do?

The Master is the connection to your Holy Guardian Angel / Daemon / Perfected Self/ Higher Self / Ascended Master/ Watcher or whatever name you choose to call it. You can use the image of the Servant as a gateway to communication with the HGA. Offerings and prayer work very effectively, as does carrying the sigil on your person or using it as a focus in concentration exercises.

Meditation upon the image of the card, or sigil, along with the intention to make contact with your Higher Being can be highly effective.

A great way to allow the energy of The Master into your life is to surrender to him and allow him to instruct and guide you on the right path. Remember The Master is **you**, so you are not bowing down or worshipping an external divine being, you are simply acknowledging your own divinity in its most complete and perfected form.

MANTRA: *I am complete and total.*

KEY WORDS:
Ascended, Divine, Complete, Wisdom, Guidance, Best Version, Evolved, Surrender, Holy, Mystical, Sacred, Spiritual, Mastery.

THE MASTER PRAYER:
Oh, great Servant The Master,
who has learned every lesson and solved every puzzle,
show me how to see things as you do
so that I make the perfect choice and take the correct road.
May I become what I am destined to become.

The Media

This Servant shows us how to get the word out about things that are important to us. It encourages us to always remember the power of propaganda – both good and bad.

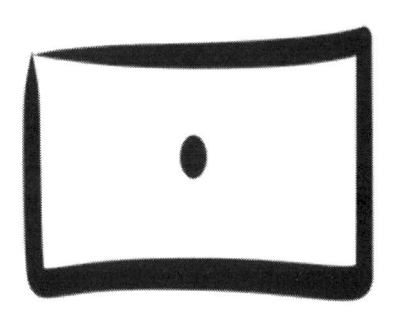

When The Media appears it is a warning that everything is not as it seems. You are being fed a story that isn't the full truth, or has been spun to make one side look more favorable than the other.

The story that is being presented has been designed to create a certain reaction or response. This version of the truth may be presented in order to fool you or it may be that someone is trying to spare your feelings about something. Either way, the whole truth is not being told. Things are probably not as they seem, there is a level of spin, lies, manipulation and fraud. The story isn't an outright lie or falsehood however, some elements are in fact the truth. It has just been presented in a way that distorts the full truth of the situation.

The Media may also suggest that you are being

influenced by outside forces to think or believe a certain way, and it is up to you to try to work out the real truth of the situation. The world around you may not be exactly as you think. The Media calls for you to make your own judgments about events and not rely so heavily on other people's opinions and life views.

In a reading The Media can sometimes suggest that someone is slandering or spreading gossip or lies about you. Also very much a reminder that you shouldn't believe everything you hear, read or see on the internet, newspapers, or on TV.

The Media represents propaganda and half-truths, whereas The Moon would suggests outright lies and falsehoods.

The Media can be used to help see the truth of a situation, to distinguish the spin from the truth or to get a better feel, or read, of a situation or event.

The Media is also useful in propaganda and self-promotion, to help gain publicity or in "getting the word out". The Media can be extremely useful in getting a good image of you or your product presented to the world. It can also help restore your good name after a period of it being tarnished. Highly effective in generating a buzz around a new project or product, and generally making the public see you in a good light.

In curse work The Media is a very useful aid to destroy the good name, or public reputation of an enemy.

MANTRA: *The good word is out.*

KEY WORDS:
Disinformation, Hype, Publicity, Advertising, Promotion, Spin, Half-truths, Falsehoods, Deception, Dishonesty, Insincere, Disingenuous, Sly, Propaganda, Public Relations.

THE MEDIA PRAYER:
Oh, great Servant The Media,
who knows the truth behind every half-truth,
show me what is correct and what is false
so that I may know who my friends and my enemies are.
May my name be in good standing

The Messenger

This Servant shows us how best to communicate. It encourages us to aim to be always open to what life may be trying to tell us.

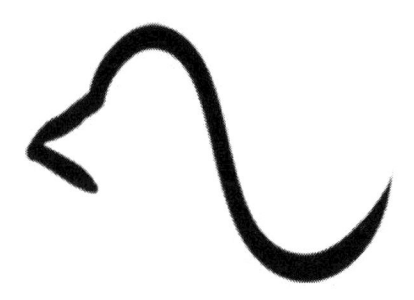

The Messenger is a sign that someone, or something, is trying to communicate with you and that perhaps you aren't giving the message your full attention. Sometimes we can be so wrapped up in an event that we just can't see the good news in front of us. However, this Servant can also be a sign that you aren't facing up to some truth that you'd prefer to ignore, or you are refusing to see someone else's point of view on a topic. Is there something that people aren't allowed to speak about to you? Are there topics that you refuse to talk about? Are there areas of your life that you won't discuss with others?

The Messenger is a general indicator for you to listen, and become more open to the communication going on around you. Try to make sure that you are heeding, receiving and being receptive to all messages that are coming your way. Someone is trying to tell you something, but are you listening?

The Messenger is useful for any magick work that involves communications, such as sending or receiving emails, giving talks or presentations, any sort of public speaking, writing blogs, or any sort of journalism. Also helpful when trying to get through to someone on a particular topic or idea. This Servant can be used to get people talking again after arguments, or when communication between two parties breaks down.

The Messenger is also effective in finding a channel to get a message to someone whom you have been long out of touch with and are not sure how to contact again. It is even useful when the other person is refusing to communicate with you. To ask The Messenger to deliver a message, simply write it down on a piece of paper, fold it over and put the person's name on it. Then make a candle offering to The Messenger in front of its image or sigil. When the candle has burned down nearly completely use the flame to burn the paper with your message written on it. Then blow or throw the remaining ash into the wind.

MANTRA: *All that is spoken is heard.*

KEY WORDS:
Communication, News, Notice, Connection, Contact, Conversation, Listening, Delivery, Link, Correspondence, Receiving.

THE MESSENGER PRAYER:
Oh, great Servant The Messenger,
who allows all things to speak to each other,
let my communication arrive swiftly
so that the words I express are received and understood.
May all messages be received.

The Monk

This Servant shows us how to keep our lives simple and uncomplicated. He encourages us to spend more time in meditation, introspection and contemplation.

When the Monk appears in a reading it can be a sign that you are overloading your life with too much "stuff" and the best course of action would be to simplify, and uncomplicate your life a bit.

The Monk calls for silence, calm, relaxation and time spent away from the rat race. The Monk suggests that you spend time in simplicity, perhaps meditating, doing some introspection or contemplative exercises designed to slow you down and focus on the now. Turn off the outer world for a while and come back to the simple inner world.

The Monk suggests that a period of quiet and calm may be the best medicine for what ails you. Quiet time without TVs, mobile devices or the internet may be called for, along with some long walks out alone in nature, or doing simple things that you enjoy doing just for enjoyment's sake - not to learn, not to better yourself, not to get ahead - just to for the delight of the act itself..

The Monk asks you "do you need all the 'stuff' that you have surrounded yourself with or could you let go of some of it?"

The Monk can be used any time you want to enter into a period of peace, calm or simplicity. A very favorable Servant to keep an image of in your meditation area. A quick prayer or offering before your meditation practice can also be extremely beneficial.

If life is getting a bit too much or complicated for you – if you find yourself surrounded by too much *stuff* or drama then an invocation of The Monk can be very beneficial in starting to make your life more simple and quiet.

Utilising The Monk in banishing rituals to rid the operator's life of needless baggage can be extremely beneficial.

MANTRA: *All is calm, all is good.*

KEY WORDS:
Simplicity, Ease, Decluttered, Natural, Quiet, Serene, Peaceful, Meditation, Calm, Harmonious, Relaxed, Composed, Placid, Tranquil, Gentle.

THE MONK PRAYER:
Oh, great Servant The Monk,
who lives and moves in serene simplicity,
show me how to declutter and destress my life

---

so that I can relaxed and become calm and at ease.
May all beings know peace.

The Moon

This Servant shows us that which is hidden in the darkness. It encourages us to acknowledge our self-deceptions, while also being mindful of the lies told by others, and the general illusions of life.

The Moon is about hope. In the darkness of the black night The Moon will shower us with her gentle illumination. The Moon is the light at the end of the tunnel. But a word of caution: Hope can set you up for a big fall. Hope is a dangerous thing, after all. That said, hope is sometimes the only thing that can get you through the darker times of your life, and it has to be said that sometimes we get more than we ever hoped for.

The Moon often represents your 'shadow' self - the bits of you that you don't want to acknowledge. You should aim to become aware of any tendencies you may have to project fear and anxiety onto the events or people that surround you. Then try to turn this negative energy into a positive and constructive energy. Life reflects back to you your thoughts and beliefs in the same way the moon reflects the sun's light. Remember The Moon has no light of its own, it's merely reflecting the sun's light.

The Moon is a mystery and can represent a number of things depending on the question asked or the problem at hand. As The Moon has no light of its own, it can represent illusion or falseness in some aspect of the your life - is someone you know pretending to be something they are not, or are you pretending to be someone or something you aren't? This is made more likely if The Media card also appears in a reading. While The Media represents propaganda and half-truths, The Moon mostly suggests outright lies and falsehoods.

The Moon is an extremely useful Servant for seeing past the illusions of daily life, the lies people tell and of course the lies we tell ourselves. The Moon can shed light on our self-deceptions, like a beam of light shining in a darkened room. The Moon can be invoked to enable you to see what you are hiding from yourself or what falsehood your shadow self is insisting is true. You will be able to see the repressed and unknown sides of your personality that are holding you back. This can be extremely hard and tortuous work but also probably the most rewarding in terms of genuine clarity and increased happiness in life.

The Moon can help you to look past the story and lies, and see the truth. The Moon's sigil can be used during conversations or interactions to aid in seeing if someone is being deceitful or lying. Mentally push the sigil into the persons head as they talk and see if they trip up or give in and tell the truth.

The Moon works extremely well when used on the night of the full moon, as one would expect.

MANTRA: *There is always a light in the darkness.*

KEY WORDS:
Illusion, Reflection, Deception, Lies, Hope, Wish, Illumination, Shadow, Mystery.

THE MOON PRAYER:
Oh, great Servant The Moon,
who shines bright in the deepest darkness,
illuminate the path ahead of me
so that I see the truth of who and what I am.
May my hopes become reality.

The Mother

This Servant shows us all about fertility, security and nurturing. She encourages us to feel safe and secure and to be mindful of our general well-being.

The Mother comes to show you that life is offering you affection, support, nurturing and unconditional love. You are reminded that you are allowed to be whatever or whoever you want to be and all you have to do is move ever closer towards your goals.

The Mother brings a huge hug from the universe, full of acceptance, love and affection. Everything right now is ok. You can relax and feel safe in the sweet embrace of the ever loving Mother.

This Servant shows a need to be loved and looked after by life. You may be feeling the desire to be nurtured by life, and the appearance of this card suggests that this is a reality.

The Mother always heralds the birth of new things rather than the end of old things. She can be a sign of pregnancy, or the beginning of a new period in your life such as new job, new relationships or new home. The Mother represent fertility in all its different aspects. She is the embodiment of the earth elemental energy.

The Mother is to be invoked when you need to feel loved by life and you need to feel the unconditional love that is emanating from The Mother's heart.

The Mother is very useful for people wishing to conceive or start a family. Candle offerings, prayers or novenas are suggested. The Mother is also extremely helpful in all magick concerning children and family. The Mother can be enlisted to keep children safe and out of trouble, and to make sure they feel loved and appreciated. The Mother can be invoked to aid in becoming a better parent or guardian.

The Mother is useful in all types of fertility magick including money magick. As a representation of the earth element, The Mother can be invoked to help with stability, growth and strength.

MANTRA: *I am loved and supported.*

KEY WORDS:
Nurtured, Cared For, Supported, Fertility, Mothered, Loved, Acceptance, Unconditional Love, Compassion, Adored, Kept Safe, Protected, Cherished, Honored.

THE MOTHER PRAYER:
Oh, great Servant The Mother,
who gave birth to us all and keeps us safe,
take me in your warm embrace
so that I feel your love, compassion and protection.
May all feel secure.

The Opposer

This Servant shows us how we are being restricted by outside forces. He encourages us to face the opposition and restrictions imposed on us by others.

When The Opposer appears it is an indication that you are being restricted by outside forces or influences. Someone or something is stopping you from getting your way - this could be laws, social customs, family obligations or traditions or social pressure, but often represents an actual person in your life.

Although they both deal with restriction or limiting, The Devil points at restrictions from within yourself, while The Opposer is about restrictions coming from outside forces.

You can overcome this resistance but the victory can only be achieved by action- it will not resolve itself if ignored. There must be some form of a battle with the opposing force for the oppression to cease. The Opposer will never back down unless confronted and even then events may get worse before a solution is found. This may result in the need for you to walk away - but not always; this isn't a card of failure or defeat. It's just a sign that a battle is ahead and you must prepare yourself for that.

The Opposer reminds you that for the most part these restrictions aren't actually real in an absolute sense, but going against them will usually come with a penalty or punishment. For instance, you can drive your car at any speed you desire, but if you get caught going too fast in a restricted area you will have to face the consequences and pay the fine.

The Opposer can be banished when someone appears in your life that is getting in your way, messing with your plans, or is placing some sort of restrictions on you. Drawing The Opposer's sigil along with writing your target person's name on a stone and then throwing it into the sea or a river is a great banishing .As is writing the person's name along with The Opposer's sigil on paper and then burning it.

In baneful magick, The Opposer can be sent to restrict an enemy in their plans. Also useful when trying to stop new laws being created, or to stop decisions being made. Also useful for restricting planning permission or permits.

MANTRA: *Nothing can oppose me.*

KEY WORDS:
Oppressed, Restricted, Limited, Opposition, Hostility, Competition, Conflict, Struggle, Clash,

Contrariety, Contention, Obstruction, Duel, Enemy, Adversary, Antagonist, Hindrance.

THE OPPOSER PRAYER:
Oh, great Servant The Opposer,
who sets us restrictions and challenges,
remove your influence (or representative) from my life
so that I can get these things I want.
May I no longer be obstructed.

The Planet

This Servant shows us our place in creation. It encourages us to remember just how immense and awe inspiring the universe is.

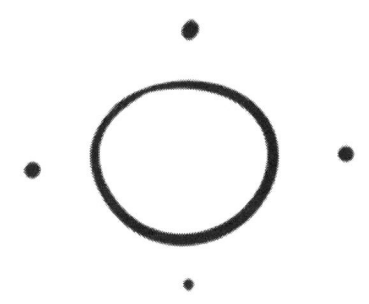

The Planet suggests that you try to view life in the cosmic sense for a moment and try to see the huge tapestry and wonder of creation. The Planet asks you to ponder what it is all about.

The Planet moves 'round the universe in a precise orbit and trajectory. It reminds you of the patterns of life and the different seasons that they must go through. The universe is a vast and ancient place and has experienced more than humans could possibly imagine. You must remember that you are as much a part of creation as the planets, the solar systems, the suns, and the galaxies. You are a child of the stars and you should try to remember that when life seems not worth living or worth the effort.

However, if you are starting to take yourself too seriously or feeling that you are of immense importance to the universe, or humanity as a whole, then The Planet arrives to remind you that your life, while part of the great whole, is just a tiny, tiny fraction of it and no matter what you do or achieve it doesn't really compare to anything on the grand scale of things. The Planet reminds you to be aware of your individual insignificance and to stop claiming to be more than they actually are.

The Planet wants you to be aware of what you have captured in your own atmosphere and gravitational pull. Is everything in your personal orbit helpful and useful, or have you surrounded yourself with junk or negativity? Extra note should be taken of this idea if The Planet appears with The Monk.

The Planet is an extremely useful Servant in rituals where you need to feel extremely big and powerful or where massive results are needed. The Planet is the Servant of manifesting as The Planet's gravity can pull to it anything that is needed. But always keep in mind just how easy it is to clutter up the atmosphere with useless stuff.

The Planet can be used in banishing rituals to clear your orbit of useless debris and junk that you have accumulated over the years. Very useful in all banishing type rituals.

The Planet can also be used to see the patterns and seasons of life. Invoke The Planet to see the orbits and patterns that the operator is spinning around in. If you find that you are just repeating patterns over and over again, use The Planet to break the cycle.

MANTRA: *I am part of the great all.*

KEY WORDS:
Manifesting, Gravity, Awe, Importance, Scale, Size, Huge, Your Place in the World, Patterns, Bigger Picture, Embody, Force, Pull, Clutter, Surroundings, Immensity, Power.

THE PLANET PRAYER:
Oh, great Servant The Planet,
who has been around since the beginning of it all,
show me the immenseness and wonder of the universe
so that I may know the miracle of creation .
May my eyes be opened.

The Protector

This Servant shows us how to protect ourselves and our loved ones from harm. It encourages us to value protection, security and safety.

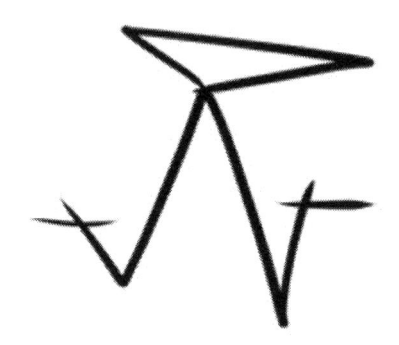

When The Protector appears it is a sign that protection and security is, or should be a concern for you. While it's not a call to become overly paranoid about security issues, The Protector does suggest that you should make an effort to keep yourself out of harm's way, or to refrain from making any foolish moves that could land you in trouble.

The Protector can also be a sign that someone is looking out for you or protecting you from behind the scenes. The Protector can easily denote a guardian person such as a parent, partner or law officer.

In a divination, the true implications of this card, more than a lot of the others, will be best known by the cards appearing around it or by the question asked.

The Protector is the go to servant for any time you feel you are in danger or your safety has been compromised. The sigil can be drawn in the mind's eye, or in the air in front of you, as a real time strategy during occasions when you feel the need for extra protection.

The Protector can also be sent to events and occasions in the future (such as vacation time, for safe travel), or to protect particular items. Keeping the sigil on your person at all times will aid in ongoing protection. Placing the sigil over the main door to serve as protection for the household is equally helpful.

Candle offerings to The Protector are helpful in returning curses or magical attacks back to the sender.

MANTRA: *Everything is secure, I am safe.*

KEY WORDS:
Protection, Safety, Security, Defend, Secure, Guard, Shielded, Safeguard, Keep Safe, Out of Harm's Way.

THE PROTECTOR PRAYER:
Oh, great Servant The Protector,
who keeps all things safe and secure from evil,
protect me from all harms and attacks
so that I may walk freely and safely through the world .
May all be protected and safe.

The Protester

This Servant shows us how to fight against injustice. She encourages us to speak our minds, push for what we think is right, and never back down.

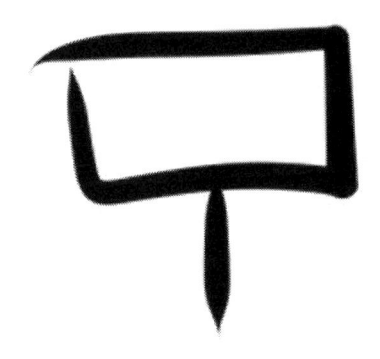

The Protester appears when you feel that your concerns aren't being listened to. You feel an injustice and no longer want to stand idly by and let it happen. The Protester embodies directed anger and frustration against that which you are facing. This Servant calls to you to do more than just be angry or outraged at events - it suggests that you should use this powerful energy to effect change.

This Servant can also appear when you feel a great injustice has occurred or that you are being oppressed or restricted. If this Servant appears together with The Opposer, The Media, The Moon, The Devil or similar Servants then it is a sign that you have to start standing up for yourself or else you will be crushed and unheard.

This Servant appears when things have become

unacceptable and the time has come for action and change. It can suggest an argument or disagreement is in store or some sort of injustice is likely to occur that is likely to enrage or upset you.

The Protester is a Servant encompassing the energy of Mars, the God of War. This Servant is extremely useful if you need to go into battle or win a fight. Invoking The Protester is extremely useful during business negotiations, circumstances that require a strong hand, or before actual physical fights. Also very useful in sports and games.

The Protester is also extremely useful in turning anger and rage into a powerful force of change rather than into frustration. The sigil can be used to channel angry energy into healthier outlets such as exercise, increasing ambition, goal setting, or self-determination.

In baneful work The Protester can be made to aid in encouraging dissent in fellow work mates, friends or the general public, or to enlist them to your cause.

MANTRA: *I will be heard.*

KEY WORDS:
Protest, Bellicose, Challenge, Demonstration, Dissent, Objection, Outcry, Revolt, Anger, Shouting, Grievance, Gripe, Howl, Rally, Insist, Resist.

THE PROTESTER PRAYER:
Oh, great Servant The Protester,

who always stands her ground and is heard,
lend me your vicious and powerful voice
so that I too can be heard and listened to.
May nothing stand in my way.

The Road Opener

This Servant shows us how to clear, banish and remove the obstacles in our path. He encourages us to recognise the opportunities that are appearing around us.

When The Road Opener appears it is a sign that the future is going to lead to new and interesting places. New opportunities are now becoming available, and an improvement in job, love or financial prospects is literally on the horizon.

The Road Opener is a sign that the way ahead is clear and that you should pursue your goals with all your might as nothing can now stop you from achieving what you want.

The Road Opener can also be a sign that an obstacle that was once in your way has now been removed (or in the case of a future card - will be) and you are now better fixed to move forward. The Road Opener is always a positive sign of better things to come.

The Road Opener can be used to open new

paths or for clearing obstacles from existing paths. These paths can be career, relationship, creative, or any area that you want to become more free to pursue. You can ask The Road Opener to create new opportunities for you or to show you avenues of interest that you might not have previously considered but which would suit you well and bring you great enjoyment. Candle offerings are very useful, as is drawing the sigil in the air and breathing or pushing it into job applications, CVs or résumés.

If someone or something is standing in your way The Road Opener can be enlisted to help in the removal of this obstacle. A form or aspect of the great god Ganesha appears above the open road and He is known as the great remover of obstacles. Chanting "*Aum Gam Ganapataye Namaha*" over the Servant's image while seeing your block or obstacle dissolve can be extremely effective.

A general road opening working could be done to open any suitable paths, which can lead to some unexpected but amazing new directions.

MANTRA: *The road ahead is clear.*

KEY WORDS:
Opening, Banishing, Clearing, Removing, Opportunities, Dispel, Luck, Favorable Circumstances, Improved Probability of Success, Advantage, New Directions, Lucky Break, Prosperity, New Focus.

THE ROAD OPENER PRAYER:
Oh, great Servant The Road Opener,
who removes all obstacles from the path,
let the road ahead of me be open
so that I move into new success, opportunities and growth.
May all my paths be clear.

The Saint

This Servant shows us how to ask for help. He encourages us to seek out experts who are more equipped than us for the task at hand, or who can intercede on our behalf.

When The Saint appears it is a sign that you might be best served by asking someone to intercede on your behalf rather than going directly yourself. For instance, you may benefit from someone putting a good word in with a prospective boss before applying for the job or making contact yourself.

If an argument has occurred between you and someone else, The Saint suggests that the best course of action is to ask a mutual third party to help smooth things over with the other person first before you talk to them yourself.

The Saint also suggests that it is often better to use an expert than try to do something yourself. Using an expert may be more expensive in the short term but will save you a lot more in the long term. The best person for the job at hand is someone who knows exactly what they are doing and have experience in dealing with similar cases. Now is not the time to try to learn a new skill.

The Saint is the patron of magick and can lend his power to you when tasks that would be normally out of your ability range need to be performed.

If a person, a spirit, a demon or similar has not answered your call or requests for assistance, you can ask The Saint to help make contact and put in a good word for you. The Saint is often used as the first Servant who then introduces you to the rest of the Servants.

The Saint can intercede for you in presenting your goals, prayers, wishes, healing requests, or any other needs to the higher powers. If you feel that your prayers aren't being heard, or your magick isn't as effective as it should be, then an offering in front of The Saint's image is suggested to ask him to help you get *the powers that be* listening to you.

The Saint can also intercede with other people - if you need someone to warm to you, you can send The Saint in advance to help make the target more receptive and welcoming.

MANTRA: *Pray for me.*

KEY WORDS:
Intercession, Experts, Petition, Intervention. Mediation, Prayer, Request, On Your Behalf, Favour, Adept, Experienced, Skilled, Professional, Qualified.

THE SAINT PRAYER:
Oh, great Servant The Saint,
the great patron of magick and magicians,
place a good word in the ears of the powers that be,
so that I may more easily get their attention.
May my prayers be heard.

The Seer

This Servant shows us how to use our intuition and inner guidance system. She encourages us to always go with our gut instincts.

When The Seer appears it is a sign for you to trust your gut and follow your instinct rather than try to work out the problem at hand using analytical methods. You should feel rather than think your way to the solution.

If a big decision is to be made, The Seer suggests that you should go with what feels best rather than what may be logically best. A job with less money and fewer future prospects might be a better fit for you long-term than a high paid job with prospects for advancement, for instance. You know in your heart what the right decision is and it is often the opposite of what appears to be the best decision. If you have to make a choice between two directions in life and you want to really know what your gut decision is then just toss a coin in the air to decide. However, while the coin is in the air take notice of which side you **want** the coin to land on. That is the direction you actually want to go in and The Seer is telling you to follow it. The actual side the coin lands on is irrelevant.

The Seer suggests that you should feel your way through life for a while rather than trying to mentally work out the best move available or rigidly planning.

The Seer is also about going with the flow and seeing what happens. Letting life lead you for a time, rather than pushing against it and trying to mold it into your vision. The Seer suggests that you sit back from the driving seat and see where the natural currents and tides of your life bring you.

The Seer can be used to increase your intuition, sensitivities, or emotional guidance system. Invoking The Seer can aid you in becoming more in touch with the energies around you, and give you a better feel of the surrounding events/people/problems from an intuitive level rather than an intellectual one.

The Seer is a wonderful Servant to use when you feel you are over-thinking decisions or problems. Candle offerings in return for help with getting in touch with the inner-knowing power can be extremely beneficial.

Invoke The Seer during any time that you need to *feel* rather than *think* your way through something.

MANTRA: *I feel the truth.*

KEY WORDS:

Intuition, Hunch, Clairvoyance, Discernment, Going With Your Gut, ESP, Feelings, Perception, Presentiment, Premonition, Innate Knowledge, Intuitiveness, Sixth Sense, Second Sight, Instinct, Vibes.

THE SEER PRAYER:
Oh, great Servant The Seer,
who teaches that all the guidance we need is within,
show me how to improve my intuitive sense,
so that I may know what the right decision is.
May my perception be true and accurate.

The Sun

This Servant shows us how to shine in all areas of our lives. It encourages us to realise the magnitude of our own energy, power, and radiance.

The Sun is all about power and energy. When it appears it is a sign that you are in or about to enter a period of high power, vitality, and success. The Sun suggests radiance, abundance, strength, luck, wellness, health, enthusiasm, success and enlightenment. It is a great Servant to see as it always heralds excellent times.

All power on this planet comes from The Sun, the same for growth and light. The Sun Servant tells you that you have a huge source of power available to you and now is the time to start utilising it.

The Sun Servant can be used to increase your spiritual or physical energy, for personal growth and for the increase of light in all areas of their life. Invoking The Sun Servant when weakness is felt or extra power is needed is extremely effective.

The Sun Servant can also be used to illuminate

areas or events that are occulted to you. Petition The Sun to show that which is hidden in the darkness, or for illumination on a topic which eludes you. The Sun is helpful to invoke during exercise, weight-lifting and sporting events to draw power directly from the source.

The Sun can be used to boost the power and effectiveness of other Servants or any magickal ritual. It can add power, potency, and energy to any endeavor, ritual, person, idea or event.

A very powerful servant.

MANTRA: *The light shines on all.*

KEY WORDS:

Power, Energy, Growth, Light, Heat, Force, Intensity, Potential, Strength, Dynamism, Vigor, Potency, Stamina, Vitality.

THE SUN PRAYER:
Oh, great Servant The Sun,
who gives potency and energy to all the numerous things,
let me borrow your immense strength and power
so that I am highly charged with your force and intensity.
May I always have vigor and vitality.

The Thinker

This Servant shows us how to solve problems using our analytical and rational mind. He encourages us to always go with what is logically correct rather than relying on what our hearts may be saying.

The problem you face will be best solved using reason and deduction. The Thinker is a sign that you need to put aside any emotional feelings or needs you have for the time being, and instead try to focus on the rational and intellectual thoughts instead.

There is a time to feel your way through life and there is a time to really think things through, and The Thinker instructs you that now is a time to think rather than intuit. What is the most rational way out of the problem? What will be best long-term even if it feels bad in the short-term? What is the clever move here? What is the most intelligent next step?

The Thinker wants you to think everything through rather than act on impulse or emotion. The right solution may not be the answer you want to hear but it is the most logical, and the one that should bring you the best long-term results. The Thinker requires you not to be fooled by your emotions but instead to really think about what is the wisest path to take.

The Thinker Servant can be used for problem solving using logic or when a decision needs to be made but the process is being clouded by your emotions. The Thinker can help you realise what the best and most astute way forward is.

You can invoke The Thinker in times when emotions are running high and a calm logical mind is needed. The sigil placed in the air in front of you, either mentally or physically, can aid in cutting down the high emotions of a situation or event and allow you to see what is in front of you rationally and intellectually.

MANTRA: *All is logical and coherent.*

KEY WORDS:
Astute, Intelligent, Rational, Bright, Brainy, Brilliant, Wise, Analytical, Deliberate, Impartial, Cohesion, Enlightened, Judicious, Logical, Levelheaded, Lucid, Prudent, Sane, Sober, Objective.

THE THINKER PRAYER:
Oh, great Servant The Thinker,
who sees the logic and reason behind all events,
lend me your steady eye and astute mind

so that I can make the wisest and best decision.
May logic and understanding light my way.

The Witch

This Servant shows us how to do sorcery and conjure. She encourages us to see the mystery and magic of life.

When The Witch appears in a reading it is a sign that there is a touch of magick in the air. The Witch tells you to become aware of the sense that something wyrd is at play that seems to have a life and volition of its own. Something special is happening or about to happen to you- something that may seem strange and unusual at first but will leave you with a sense of wonder. People, events or things may appear suddenly in your life as if by magick, or you will find yourself perfectly in the right place at the right time. Events will magically fall into place and good luck will abound.

The Witch leaves you with a sense of wonder, just like a knowing smile or wink from the universe. Magick is at play, and it is a joy to behold, so make sure you watch out for it.

In extreme circumstances The Witch can be a

sign that something malevolent is working against you. Look to the other cards in the reading for clarification.

The Witch Servant is useful in almost any situation. Any magick, ritual or working can be increased in potency by including or invoking The Witch. She is by a long stretch the factotum of the Servants. The Witch can also teach you magick. Candle offerings as a thanks is suggested when asking The Witch for knowledge or help. She is also a fan of rum, tobacco, herbs, oils and spices and these can be used as anoffering for any work she completes for you.

The Witch sigil can be used in real time to add magick to any event, person or problem - most effectively done by drawing it in the air with the first finger of the left hand or with a wand. The sigil is very useful for enchanting items, banishing energy (visualise the sigil in front and around you blocking any negative energy from getting to you) and in general protection magick.

Invoke The Witch to feel the magick of the surrounding area, increase potency or to get in the correct frame for ritual. The Witch is the most versatile of all the Servants and is extremely proficient in all areas. If you are ever unsure of what Servant would be the best for your particular issue you won't go far wrong by enlisting The Witch's help.

MANTRA: *I feel the magick.*

KEY WORDS:

Magic, Alchemy, Allurement, Bewitchment,
Conjuring, Devilry, Occultism, Incantation,
Mystery, Mystification, Power, Enigma, Strange,
Secret, Wyrd, Preternatural, Extraordinary,
Miraculous.

THE WITCH PRAYER:

Oh, great Servant The Witch,
who has the power to do anything she desires,
help me escape my current dilemma
so that I once again see the magick and *wyrd* of life.
May my magick be as great as yours.

The Unifying Sigil
This symbol brings all the power of the combined Servants together.

This sigil is used to connect with The Forty Servants as a whole and to connect with all the people around the world who use the Forty Servants. A must for group work. Not part of the deck per se but a symbol that can represent the entire Servant system. You can find a printable version of it at http://www.theFortyServants.com

ABOUT THE AUTHOR

Tommie Kelly is an Irish Artist and Writer, but not always in that order. He used to describe himself as the World's Only Consulting Occultist, but people didn't get the reference and thought he was being serious, so he doesn't do that now. At gun point he would describe himself as a Chaos Magician, but he isn't overly fond of labels as their function seems to be mostly about limiting things or putting them in boxes. He has had a lifelong interest in all things Occult and in Spirituality, and his only actual qualifications are in Holistic Health Studies, being qualified in Aromatherapy, Reflexology, Holistic Massage, Indian Head Massage and Reiki, but he doesn't practice any of it these days other than personal use Aromatherapy which he finds extremely pleasant and helpful.

You can keep up to date with him at http://www.AdventuresInWooWoo.com which is home to his art, writing, podcast, videos and art store.

Printed in Great Britain
by Amazon